Be My
Disciples

Christ in the
LITURGY

Peter M. Esposito
President

Jo Rotunno, MA
Publisher

James Spurgin, MA
Project Editor

Be My Disciples Program Advisors
Michael P. Horan, PhD
Elizabeth Nagel, SSD

BeMyDisciples.com

RCL
Benziger

Cincinnati, Ohio

"The Subcommittee on the Catechism, United States Conference of Catholic Bishops, has found the doctrinal content of this series, copyright 2014, to be in conformity with the *Catechism of the Catholic Church*."

NIHIL OBSTAT
Rev. Msgr. Robert Coerver
Censor Librorum

IMPRIMATUR
† Most Reverend Kevin J. Farrell, DD
Bishop of Dallas
March 5, 2013

The *Nihil Obstat* and *Imprimatur* are official declarations that the material reviewed is free of doctrinal or moral error. No implication is contained therein that those granting the *Nihil Obstat* and *Imprimatur* agree with the contents, opinions, or statements expressed.

Acknowledgments

Excerpts are taken and adapted from the *New American Bible* with Revised New Testament and Revised Psalms ©1991, 1986, 1970, Confraternity of Christian Doctrine, Washington, D.C., and are used by permission of the copyright owner. All Rights Reserved. No part of the *New American Bible* may be reproduced in any form without permission in writing from the copyright owner.

Excerpts from Second Vatican Council, *Dei Verbum*,[Dogmatic Constitution on Divine Revelation], *Lumen Gentium* [Dogmatic Constitution on the Church], *Ad Gentes* [Decree on the Mission Activity of the Church], *Christus Dominus* [Decree Concerning the Pastoral Office of Bishops in the Church] 38, *Unitatis Redintegratio* [Decree on Ecumenism] 3; Excerpt from *Gratissimam Sane*, [Letter to Families], Pope John Paul II (2 February 1994); Excerpt from *Deus Caritas Est* [God Is Love], Introduction, Pope Benedict XVI, 25 December, 2005.

English translation of the *Catechism of the Catholic Church* for use in the United States of America, second edition, ©1997, United States Catholic Conference, Inc. Used with permission. All rights reserved. Excerpts taken from *Catechists in Formation: Introduction to Theological Studies: Book 2,* Peter Ries, McGraw-Hill Inc., U.S.; Second Edition, Mission Hills, CA: Benziger Pub. Co., ©1995. Used with permission. Excerpts are taken or adapted from the English translation of the *Rite of Baptism for Children; Prayer of Consecration at the Ordination of Priest*, © 1969, International Commission on English in the Liturgy, Inc. (ICEL). All rights reserved.

Excerpts are taken or adapted from the English translation of the *Roman Missal* © 2010, International Commission on English in the Liturgy, Inc. (ICEL). All rights reserved. No part of these works may be reproduced or transmitted in any form without the permission in writing from the copyright holder.

Toll Free 877-275-4725
Fax   800-688-8356

Visit us at www.RCLBenziger.com
and BeMyDisciples.com

20789 ISBN 978-0-7829-1651-5 (Student Edition)
20793 ISBN 978-0-7829-1655-3 (Catechist Edition)
20797 ISBN 978-0-7829-1659-1 (Teacher Edition)

3rd Printing.
October 2014.

CONTENTS

Welcome to

Be My Disciples

Christ in the Liturgy

Jesus invites you to be his disciple. He wants you to know him better, to understand his message, and to follow his way of life. During this course of study, you will explore the mystery of the Church. You will learn more about what it means to take responsibility for being a member of the Body of Christ and to serve the Church in her mission.

You will also gain deeper insight into the ways that prayer and the Sacraments bind you more closely to Christ and the Church. The knowledge you gain about the Church and the Sacraments will bear fruit and make a difference in your life if you cooperate with the grace of the Holy Spirit You will learn how the life of the Church empowers you in your call to be a disciple of Jesus Christ.

Beginning Reflections

The glorified Lord lives today in the Church. In the weeks ahead you will come to know more about the Church and her sacramental life. You will deepen your understanding of how we are made sharers in the Paschal Mystery.

Consider the following reflections. Jot down your initial responses. This reflection time will help you open your mind and heart to experience the grace and power of the Holy Spirit, who will help you live as a disciple of Jesus Christ.

1 *Through Baptism you were joined to Christ and became a member of the Church, the Body of Christ.*

I will follow Christ, the Head of the Church, more faithfully and look to God with wonder and awe when

_____

_____

_____

_____

_____

_____

_____

_____

_____

_____

2 *Listen attentively to the Scripture readings during Mass. Take one of the readings that you have heard and make it part of your daily life.*

One thing that I can do to live the Word of God is

_____

_____

_____

3 *Participate fully and consciously in the Eucharistic celebration of the Mass. Having shared in the mystery of Holy Communion, make it part of your daily life.*

One thing that I can do to give thanks to the Father most holy is by

_____

_____

_____

4 *Listen well in class, ask questions when you do not understand, and take part enthusiastically in class activities.*

The honest effort I put into learning more about the Church's teachings could result in

_____

_____

_____

_____

5 *Imagine how you will continue to participate in the life of the Church as you mature.*

I can choose to prepare for that work now. One specific way I can do this is by

_____

_____

_____

_____

_____

_____

_____

_____

_____

_____

_____

_____

_____

Gathered as ONE

This prayer service can be used at the conclusion of the first day of class. The leader walks at the head of a procession to the prayer area, holding the Bible high for all to see. The leader opens the Bible and places it on a table in the prayer area.

Leader: Lord, we gather today as one people to celebrate the mystery of the Church. Through the gift of your Son and the sending of the Holy Spirit, you call us to light the world with faith.

All: Make us one, O Lord.

Reader 1: A reading from the first Letter of Paul to the Corinthians (*Proclaim 1 Corinthians 12:12–13.*) The word of the Lord.

All: Thanks be to God.

Reader 2: Lord, guide us to become more like Christ so that we may plant the seeds of unity, hope, and Salvation for all.

All: Make us one, O Lord.

Reader 3: Lord, help us to fully celebrate and respond to your constant, loving presence through the gift of the Sacraments.

All: Make us one, O Lord.

Reader 4: Lord, fill us with love so that we may be strengthened as the Body of Christ, the Church on Earth.

All: Make us one, O Lord.

Leader: O God, we come to you with open hearts, willing to be the people you have called us to be. Help us to shine the light of faith on the world around us as we prepare for the coming of the kingdom. We ask this in the name of Jesus, your Son.

All: Amen.

Come forward and bow in reverence before the Bible.

The Household of God

So then you are no longer strangers and sojourners, but you are fellow citizens with the holy ones and members of the household of God, built upon the foundation of the apostles and prophets, with Christ Jesus himself as the capstone. Through him the whole structure is held together and grows into a temple sacred in the Lord; in him you also are being built together into a dwelling place of God in the Spirit . EPHESIANS 2:19–22

What I Already Know

Complete the following sentences.

The Second Vatican Council was . . .

_____

_____

_____

The Church is . . .

_____

_____

_____

The Marks of the Church are . . .

_____

_____

_____

Faith Vocabulary

With a partner, take turns choosing words and defining them for each other. If there are words that neither of you can define, put a check mark next to them.

_____ discipleship

_____ piety

_____ Magisterium

_____ ecumenism

_____ Communion of Saints

_____ consecrated life

_____ contemplation

_____ Liturgy of the Hours

What I Want to Know

Write a question you have under each heading.

Sacred Scripture
What do you know about the Acts of the Apostles?

_____

_____

_____

The Church
What question do you have about a Sacrament you have not received?

_____

_____

_____

Another Question I Have

_____

_____

_____

LOOKING AHEAD
In this chapter the Holy Spirit invites you to ▶

EXPLORE how we live as members of the Church.
DISCOVER the Church alive in the world today.
DECIDE how to help build up the Body of Christ.

CHAPTER **1**

Discipleship for TODAY

▶ **What kind of person is God calling you to be?**

You have probably asked someone, "Who are you?" when you first met that person. Sometimes we need to ask ourselves who we are and who God calls us to be.

The leaders of the Church gather together to ask this same question about the Church when they meet in Rome. The Holy Spirit inspires them to focus on the values and truths that Jesus taught.

As I have loved you, so you also should love one another. This is how all will know that you are my disciples, if you have love for one another.

JOHN 13:34–35

▶ **What are some important values by which you live?**

TIMELINE

1200

1225–1274
Life of St. Thomas Aquinas

1300

1309–1376
Avignon Papacy

1347–1380
Life of St. Catherine of Siena

1370–1378
Papacy of Gregory XI

1378–1417
Western Schism

1420

Educated SAINTS

Throughout the history of the Church, the Holy Spirit calls upon women and men to think and pray deeply about what it means to be Church and to share their insights with us. Two such people were Catherine of Siena and Thomas Aquinas.

Catherine of Siena

Catherine of Siena was born in Italy in the fourteenth century. As a young child she had visions of Jesus Christ. At the age of 16, Catherine became a member of the Third Order of Saint Dominic. She visited many regions of Italy, where she was known for her ability to keep peace between cities and within the Church.

For seventy-four years, Popes had not been living in Rome but in Avignon, France. This custom caused great division in the Church. Catherine persuaded Pope Gregory XI to return to Rome from Avignon in 1377.

In a time when women did not normally read and write, Catherine was well educated and respected for her wisdom. In one of her spiritual writings she wrote, "The soul, who is lifted by a very great and yearning desire for the honor of God and the salvation of souls, begins by exercising herself...in the ordinary virtues, remaining in the cell of self-knowledge, in order to know better the goodness of God towards her... [O]nly when she has attained love, can she strive to follow and to clothe herself with the truth."

Catherine was canonized in 1461 and declared a Doctor of the Church in 1970. Her feast day is April 30.

▶ **How have you "clothed" yourself with the truth?**

Thomas Aquinas

When Thomas Aquinas was a young man, his classmates often called him "the dumb ox" because he was stocky and slow. Thomas' teacher, now known as Saint Albert the Great, knew better. "This ox will one day fill the world with his bellowing," he said. Indeed, Saint Thomas Aquinas has been called the most learned man who ever lived. Pope Pius XII said that studying Saint Thomas Aquinas's theology was the best way to understand Roman Catholic doctrine.

Thomas, born in 1225, was the seventh son of an Italian nobleman. When he was five years old, Thomas was sent to the Benedictine Abbey of Monte Cassino to be educated. He was a quiet, serious student who often asked his teachers, "Who is God?"

As a young man, Thomas shocked his parents by telling them he had decided to become a friar with the Dominicans, a mendicant order. This meant he would have to beg for his food. His family was furious, but Thomas would not change his mind. His family locked him in the family castle for a year. They tempted him with everything imaginable but could not get him to change his mind.

Thomas became a great teacher and writer. In Thomas' day, the works of the Greek philosopher Aristotle were very popular. Some in the Church feared that Aristotle's writings would undermine the teachings of the Church. Thomas eagerly read Aristotle's works and used them to help people understand their faith. He wrote the *Summa Theologica*, a collection of essays in which he blended the works of many philosophers with the teachings of the Church. Thomas' work was a monumental, intellectual achievement that constructed a new philosophy. Thomas demonstrated how reason and faith complement each other.

Thomas was canonized in 1323 and named a Doctor of the Church in 1567.

(this page) Saint Thomas Aquinas, c. 13th century; (previous page) Saint Catherine of Siena, Lombard School, c. 17th century

Disciple POWER

WISDOM
Wisdom combines both intelligence and compassion. A wise person understands the deeper meaning of something and also knows how this knowledge can be used for good.

FAITH JOURNAL

How have you incorporated both faith and reason into making a decision?

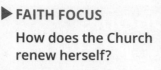

▶ **FAITH FOCUS**

How does the Church renew herself?

▶ **FAITH VOCABULARY**

aggiornamento

charism

constitutions

The First Vatican Council

In an effort to renew the Church and connect her to modern times, Pope Pius IX called Vatican Council I (1869–70). The Council addressed a number of issues, including:

1. How the Church passes on God's Revelation;

2. The teaching office of the Pope and of the college of bishops who have the **charism**, or special grace, to authentically teach in matters of faith and morals without error, and

3. The relationship between the use of faith and reason in our search to understand the meaning of God's Revelation.

Unfortunately, the Council had only completed its deliberations on the nature of the papacy and begun considerations on the other issues when in 1870 armed forces arrived outside of the doors of Saint Peter's Basilica. Pope Pius IX was forced to suspend the Council so that the bishops could return safely home. The unfinished agenda of the Vatican I Council would become an important part of the Second Vatican Council in the 20th Century.

The issues that the Council planned to discuss offered an opportunity for the first time in centuries for the Church to reflect upon what being disciples of Jesus means in the modern world. Many of the previous ecumenical councils, that is the gathering of all Catholic bishops and theologians from all over the world, were called to address a particular problem or crisis. (We will see an example of this when we study the Council of Trent in Chapter Seven.)

▶ **What do you think the Church's first priority should be today?**

Renewing the Church

The Second Vatican Council

Not quite a century would pass after the close of the First Vatican Council (1870) before Pope John XXIII (1958–1963) called the twenty-first and latest ecumenical council of the Church, the Second Vatican Council, or Vatican II.

The period between the two councils was packed with numerous developments that significantly affected the life of the Church and the world. The challenge of making the Christian message meaningful to the secular, industrialized, and technological world of the twentieth century was something of which the Church became more and more aware.

Announcement

On January 25, 1959, just three months after having been elected, Pope John XXIII announced to a small group of cardinals gathered in Rome that he had decided to call an ecumenical council of the Church. His announcement stunned not only the cardinals present but eventually the entire religious world. Everyone had expected that the early actions of this elderly Pope would be minor and transitional in nature.

Preparations

In calling this council, Pope John XXIII said that one of its primary purposes was **aggiornamento**, which is, bringing the Church up to date. He consulted bishops throughout the world about what they thought the agenda of the Council should include. The pilgrim Church was on the verge of another major renewal.

Sign of Christ

The Church exists to be a sign of Christ's presence to people in every age and culture. She acts as a sign of God's love to all humanity. Like a giant neon marquee, she must be visible for all to see. How, then, does the Church act as a sign of God's love and unity? The Church does so by acting like Christ in concrete ways to people of every time, race, and social condition. Just as Christ was visible and active among the people of his time, the Church does the same and is an effective sign that makes Jesus come alive today.

Faith CONNECTION

What ideas do you have to help the Church continue to meet the needs of today?

DID YOU KNOW?

By using the Italian word *aggiornamento*, which means "bringing up to date," to describe the work of Vatican II, Saint John XXIII renewed and deepened our understanding of the Church's relationship to the world. He said that the Church must "open the windows" and let in the fresh air of renewal if she is to preach the Gospel effectively to the men and women of the modern world.

A New Pentecost

The actual work of the Second Vatican Council took place over a period of four years, beginning with Pope John XXIII in 1962 and ending with Pope Paul VI in 1965. During this time working sessions were held in the fall of each of the four years that the Council was held.

The Council's work, as specified by the Pope, was primarily to address the pastoral renewal of the Church. He repeatedly urged Catholics to pray that the Council would be a "new Pentecost." He hoped the Council would foster the internal reform and renewal of the Church as well as the unity of all Christians.

When John XXIII died between the first and second sessions of the Council, many thought the Council would die with him. However, his successor, Pope Paul VI, proved to be a staunch promoter of John XXIII's vision and the work of the Second Vatican Council. The new Pope immediately announced his intention to continue the work of the Council.

In his opening address at the second session, Pope Paul VI listed four goals that he saw for the Council:

- Deepen people's understanding of the nature of the Church, especially the collaboration between the bishops and the Pope.

- Promote reform within the Church, especially in the liturgy.

- Foster the cause of Christian unity.

- Enter into dialogue with the modern world.

The sessions of the Second Vatican Council under his leadership worked diligently to provide the direction for the Church to achieve these goals.

▶ How did Pope Paul VI's goals for Vatican II reinforce Pope John XXIII's goal?

Official Teachings

Soon after the opening of the Council it became clear that there were many different opinions among the bishops. Nonetheless, the climate of dialogue and debate that characterized Vatican II was extraordinarily invigorating. The results of their dialogue and debate were formulated in sixteen documents.

Among the documents of the Council, four major documents, called **constitutions**, were promulgated, or officially adopted. These were the Constitution on the Sacred Liturgy [*Sacrosanctum Concilium*], the Dogmatic Constitution on the Church [*Lumen Gentium*], the Dogmatic Constitution on Divine Revelation [*Dei Verbum*], and the Pastoral Constitution on the Church in the Modern World [*Gaudium et Spes.*]. In addition, the Council approved twelve other documents, namely, nine decrees and three declarations.

Work of the Church

The Dogmatic Constitution on the Church is also called *Lumen Gentium*, which is Latin for "Light of the Nations," the opening words of the document. Through this document, the Church teaches that the work of the Church is the responsibility of all the baptized—laypeople, the ordained, and members of the consecrated life.

The Holy Spirit generously distributes charisms to all the baptized. A charism is "a specific gift or grace of the Holy Spirit which directly or indirectly

benefits the Church, given in order to help a person live out the Christian life, or to serve the common good in building up the Church" (Glossary, *Catechism of the Catholic Church*).

By cooperating with the Holy Spirit and using our gifts, we contribute in our unique ways to build up the Church on Earth and to prepare for the coming of the Kingdom of God. In our homes, workplaces, schools, and communities the Church must let her light shine.

Faith CONNECTION

How do you share your unique gifts with others?

The Truth of God's Word

The Church teaches, "Easy access to Sacred Scripture should be provided for all the Christian faithful (Dogmatic Constitution on Divine Revelation [*Dei Verbum*] 22). And all of Scripture is to be accepted as teaching the truth that God intended for the sake of Salvation (DV 11). The Bible is to be read prayerfully and carefully. We do this by studying the language and types of writing the human authors of the Bible used.

Most importantly, the Church reminds us that a Catholic's spiritual life stands on two "legs" — the regular reception of Holy Communion and the regular reading and studying of the Bible. We can better understand the meaning of Scripture when we read it, study it, and pray over it with the Church.

Deepening the Faith

In 1985 Pope John Paul II called together the bishops on the twentieth anniversary of the Second Vatican Council. This synod of bishops studied the teachings of Vatican II. They recommended that a new catechism be developed. The work of developing the new catechism began in 1986 and concluded in 1992.

The *Catechism of the Catholic Church* systematically presents the teachings and spiritual heritage of the Catholic Church. All of the faithful now have a resource to which they can refer whenever they need to clarify or deepen their understanding of a particular aspect of Church teaching.

Faith CONNECTION

Discuss how you can use the *Catechism of the Catholic Church* to help in your faith formation.

KEEPING Faith ALIVE

We study the history of the Church to learn about our roots and to recognize that the work of the Holy Spirit has always been present within the Church. We take from the past that which will help us continue to know, love, and serve God and his people today.

You are a member of the Church of today. The virtues and qualities that our Catholic ancestors needed in order to keep their faith alive, especially in times of great conflict, are the same virtues you need today. You are living in a world where certain teachings, values, and beliefs promoted by some in the world stand in contradiction to the Gospel and the teachings of the Catholic Church. This may at times make it difficult for you to live your faith.

■ You need to ask yourself: What will help me continue to face and overcome the challenges to keeping the flame of faith alive in my life?

A **MESSENGER** IN THE **WORLD**

You are part of the Church. You make a difference in the life of the Church. So believe that you are a messenger of hope and love in the world.

Wisdom is a Gift of the Holy Spirit. Wisdom helps you see the world through the eyes of faith, to see the world as God sees it.

■ How can you grow in wisdom?

Courage, or fortitude, is also a Gift of the Holy Spirit and a Cardinal Virtue. You also need courage to live your faith. Courage is the moral and mental strength to choose what is right, even when doing so is difficult.

■ How can you overcome the fears of living your life as a follower of Christ, no matter the cost?

Perseverance flows from courage, helping your commitment to be a follower of Jesus Christ.

■ What obstacles to living the Gospel do you face that demand perseverance?

MY FAITH CHOICE

Think about wisdom, courage, and perseverance. Reflect on how one of these habits of discipleship is already strong within you.

This week I can use wisdom, courage, and perseverance by:

_____

_____.

 PRAY Holy Spirit, strengthen in me the gift of wisdom so that I will have the courage to persevere through challenges and continue to grow in faith. Amen.

Recall

Define each of these faith vocabulary terms:

1. aggiornamento _____

2. charism _____

3. constitution _____

Choose one of the questions below and write a brief paragraph to answer your choice.

4. Describe the main goals of the Second Vatican Council.

_____

_____

5. Discuss the work of the Church as described by the Dogmatic Constitution on the Church.

_____

_____

Reflect

Using what you have learned in this chapter, reflect on and describe in your own words the meaning of this statement:

Christ is the Light of nations...a light brightly visible on the countenance of the Church.

LUMEN GENTIUM, [DOGMATIC CONSTITUTION ON THE CHURCH], 1

_____

_____

Share

Discuss with a partner how your knowledge of Church teaching helps you mature in your faith.

WITH MY FAMILY

Discuss with your family how as a Catholic family you are making the light of Christ visible to others.

To Help You
REMEMBER

1. Vatican I began a deep reflection on what it means to be Church.

2. Vatican II brought a new breath of fresh air into the Church.

3. As a result of Vatican II, the Church emphasizes even more the importance of being disciples in the world.

Prayer for
RENEWAL

Leader: Come, Holy Spirit,
Advocate and Teacher,
open our minds and hearts
to hear and live the Gospel.

Reader: A reading from the Acts of the Apostles.

Proclaim Acts of the Apostles 2:1–4.

The word of the Lord.

All: **Thanks be to God.**

Leader: Let us all pray together the prayer that Pope John XXIII gave to us in his opening address to the Second Vatican Council:

All: **Renew your wonders in our time,
as though for a new Pentecost,
and grant that the holy Church,
preserving unanimous and continuous prayer,
together with Mary the Mother of Jesus,
and also under the guidance of Saint Peter,
may increase the reign of the Divine Savior,
the reign of truth and justice,
the reign of love and peace.
Amen.**

LOOKING AHEAD
In this chapter the Holy Spirit invites you to ▶

EXPLORE the Church as the People of God.
DISCOVER the main ways in which God works through us.
DECIDE on how can you serve the Church.

CHAPTER **2**

The People of GOD

▶ **To which kinds of groups do you belong?**

Belonging to groups is important to everyone. At the heart of our families and friendships is a secured sense of belonging. To belong means that each of us has a vital role in contributing to the good of the group.

Everyone who is baptized belongs to the Church. We, as members of the Body of Christ, are therefore responsible for carrying out the work of the Church.

But as it is, there are many parts, yet one body.

1 CORINTHIANS 12:20

▶ **What are the values by which you live?**

1978–1978	2005–2013	2013
Papacy of John Paul I	Papacy of Benedict XVI	Election of Pope Francis

1970   2000   2013

TIMELINE

2006 — Darfur Peace Agreement
2010 — Earthquake hits Haiti.

Global MISSION

Caritas Internationalis, the agency that coordinates more than 160 humanitarian relief activities, has incorporated a sense of belonging into its mission. Founded under the guidance of Father Lorenz Werthmann in 1895, the organization originally coordinated Catholic aid and relief activities in Germany.

Recently, the scope of the organization has become much larger. In 1947, the organization received a new name, "Caritas Catholica," to indicate it has a universal mission. The Pope endorsed the organization as the official representative of the Church for coordinating international aid to people in need in cooperation with the United Nations. In light of the importance placed on ecumenism after the Second Vatican Council, the organization is now known as Caritas Internationalis. The group was praised by Pope John Paul II for its contribution towards the goal of "globalizing solidarity."

In the United States, the work of Caritas Internationalis is carried out by its local subsidiary, Catholic Relief Services. Caritas Internationalis and all its subsidiaries coordinate the resources of a variety of international aid organizations to efficiently and quickly send help to wherever it is needed.

▶ What are some good ways to help people in need?

Efforts Today

In recent years Caritas Internationalis has been very active in the Darfur region of the nation of Sudan in Africa. Trapped between the two sides of a violent civil war and terrorized by the "janjaweed," a group of armed bandits operating in southern Sudan, the people of Darfur were driven from their homes and deprived of food and water. Through the efforts of Caritas Internationalis, many of these people have seen their lives changed for the better.

One example of their efforts includes helping the people in Hilet-Hausa who did not have access to a supply of clean running water. Caritas provided the funds and supplies for the project in which the people of the refugee camp constructed two wells equipped with solar-powered pumps.

In a refugee camp, a young mother named Maryam could not find enough food to give to her seven-month-old son. The boy, Najmeldin, had to be taken to a hospital because he was suffering from malnutrition. Fortunately, the case came to the attention of a worker based in a nutrition center sponsored by Caritas Internationalis who helped.

Success stories like these are common as Caritas International works to bring the healing and generous love of Jesus to a broken world in great need. Such people have certainly heard and responded to Jesus' call to love as he loves us.

FAITH JOURNAL

What have you done for others in response to Jesus' call?

▶ FAITH FOCUS

Who makes up the
People of God?

▶ FAITH VOCABULARY

consecrated life

laity

ordained ministry

The Plan of God

The origin of the Church lies deep within the plan of God from the very beginning of time. Part of God's plan is to share his own divine life with us. The Church is the sign and instrument of Salvation. She is the sign and instrument of our reconciliation and communion with God and with one another. The word *church* means "convocation." God's Word convokes, or gathers together, believers to form the People of God who, nourished by the Body of Christ, truly become the Body of Christ.

One enters the People of God through Baptism and the response of faith. All are called to belong to the new People of God, so that in Christ they may form one family in faith. At the end of time, all God's children will be gathered together.

The Universal Covenant

God promised to Noah a universal covenant with all people (see Genesis 9:9–13). Then God promised Abraham that he would be the father of a great nation (see Genesis 12:2). God elected the people of Israel to be his people. On Mount Sinai God gave his Law to the people of Israel through Moses. Later the prophets announced that God would make a new and everlasting covenant with all people—just as he had promised (see Jeremiah 31:31–34).

The promise of the New Covenant was instituted in Jesus Christ (see Luke 22:14–20). Jesus called his first followers to be the foundation of this new People of God. When his redemptive work was accomplished on Earth, the Risen and glorified Christ returned to his Father in Heaven. As Jesus promised, the Father sent the Holy Spirit in his name. The Holy Spirit forms the followers of Jesus into the new People of God, the Church.

▶ **What has been one of the most important journeys you have taken? Why?**

Gathered in Christ's Name

The Communion of the Church

There is a deep solidarity among the people that God has made holy by sharing his life with us. The Church is a:

- Communion in the faith: a sharing in the faith handed down from the Apostles.

- Communion in the Sacraments: a sharing in the Paschal Mystery.

- Communion in the Holy Spirit: a sharing that is enriched by spiritual gifts of the Holy Spirit.

- Communion of charity: a sharing in the building up the Church.

The Church is also a community of holy people. This communion of holy people includes.

- The faithful here on Earth
- The faithful who are being purified after death in Purgatory
- The faithful experiencing eternal and perfect communion with God and the Saints in Heaven

The Church on Earth continues to pray for those being purified after their bodily death. The Saints living in Heaven care about us and pray for us. They serve the faithful on Earth as our advocates before God in Heaven. This faith moves us to pray to them and to learn about their lives on Earth.

The Church is also known as the Communion of Saints. The Communion of Saints is a communion of all holy things and holy people that make up the Church.

Faith CONNECTION

Design an image that illustrates the Communion of Saints.

Spiritual Gifts

The visible Church on Earth is made up of many people. Each baptized person has responsibility for the mission of the Church. Joined to Christ in Baptism, all the baptized are called to share in the Paschal Mystery of Christ's Passion, Death, Resurrection, and glorious Ascension and to be happy with him forever.

The Holy Spirit blesses the People of God with charisms, gifts, and responsibilities to help build up the Body of Christ on Earth. Saint Paul wrote:

> There are different kinds of spiritual gifts but the same Spirit; there are different forms of service but the same Lord; there are different workings but the same God who produces all of them in everyone. To each individual the manifestation of the Spirit is given for some benefit.
> 1 Corinthians 12:4–7

Lights in the World

At Baptism all the newly baptized receive the gift of the Holy Spirit and are anointed with the blessed oil called Sacred Chrism. The presider prays:

> He [God the Father] now anoints you with the chrism of salvation, so that, united with his people, you may remain for ever a member of Christ who is Priest, Prophet, and King.
> Rite of Baptism 98

After the anointing the newly baptized receives a lighted candle, a symbol of Christ. They are to live as lights of Christ in the world.

Most of the baptized are members of the **laity**, or laypeople. Laypeople are called by God to place the gifts bestowed upon them by the Holy Spirit at the service of the world, so that all who they meet might more clearly experience the presence of the Risen Christ in their lives. Lay people are called by God to respectfully and charitably offer their insights and witness to the leaders of the Church as

well. Laypeople are lights of faith, hope, and love in their families and among their friends, in their communities, in their workplaces, and in their parishes. They are living witnesses for Christ at the very heart of the human community.

▶ How have some laypeople helped you discern your talents and gifts?

Ordained Ministers

Bishops, priests, and deacons are members of the ordained ministry of the Church. They are ordained to serve the whole Church. Through the **ordained ministry**, especially of bishops and priests, the presence of Christ as Head of the Church is made visible in the midst of the Church. Bishops are helped by priests, their coworkers, and by deacons in their work of teaching the faith, celebrating divine worship, and guiding the faithful entrusted to their care. All ordained ministers of the Church are members of the clergy.

▶ Which gifts do you think are necessary for a man to be a priest?

The Consecrated Life

Laypeople and ordained ministers sometimes make promises to a life of poverty, chastity, and obedience in a way approved by the Church. They can live out this **consecrated life** publicly in religious communities or even as cloistered religious, or religious who do not leave the place where they live, work, and pray. In whatever ways these members of the Church live out their vocation, they are living signs of God's saving love at work in the world. Their lives remind us to keep our focus on living the Gospel.

Faith CONNECTION

What kind of commitment do you think one needs to live the consecrated life?

Successors of the Apostles

Jesus gave his Church on Earth a structure. He chose the Twelve with Saint Peter as their head to serve the Church in his name (see John 21:15–17). The Pope is the successor of Saint Peter. The Pope is also the bishop of Rome and the head of all the bishops. He is the Vicar of Christ on Earth and has been given the ministry to care for the whole Church. He is the visible foundation and pastor of the universal Church on Earth. Bishops are the successors of the Apostles. Bishops are chosen by the Pope to lead local churches in every part of the world. As the chief pastor for his local church, a bishop serves as Christ's representative to shepherd the people in his name.

Teacher on Faith and Morals

The first duty of the bishop is to preach the Good News. Guided by the Holy Spirit, the bishops, as a successors of the Apostles, pass on, preserve, and defend the truth of the Gospel. The bishops teach authoritatively on matters of faith and morals. The faithful are called to believe what the Church teaches.

Minister of Word and Sacrament

Helped by priests, their coworkers, and by deacons, bishops sanctify the Church by their prayers and work, by their ministry of Word and Sacrament, as well as by their personal example of holiness. Bishops have the responsibility and authority to see to it that the Sacraments are celebrated reverently with the faithful in their care. Bishops are stewards of the grace of Christ, especially of the Eucharist over which they preside or delegate to priests as coworkers.

Shepherd of the Flock

The bishop leads and serves the faithful by following the example of Christ the Good Shepherd (see Luke 22:26). Those chosen to shepherd the Church as bishops are to serve others as Jesus served (see John 13:14–17). They are the sign and source of the unity of the Church in the particular church they serve.

CALLED from GOD

Each one of us has a vocation—a calling from God to live our faith in Christ in a certain way. Your vocation is that calling from God to meet the needs of your family, friends, world and the Church. Your first and most basic call is to love: love God, love yourself, and love others as Jesus taught. This love can be lived out through marriage and family life, the single life, the consecrated life as a member of a religious community, or as an ordained minister.

The word *vocation* comes from a Latin word that means "a calling." Throughout our lives, God calls each of us to follow him in a special way. How we respond to God's call is up to us. To help you respond to this call it is important for you to discover your gifts and talents. This will help you discern the best way for you to serve God and others.

PRACTICE **YOUR GIFTS**

Discernment is a prayerful way to gain insight into God's plan for you and your vocation in life. This is an ongoing process. Here are a few steps to help you discern:

■ Set aside quiet time. Ask the Holy Spirit to open your mind and heart to what God is saying to you about your life.

■ Be open to possibilities. Consider the possibility that God may be calling you to be ordained, to live in religious life, to be married, or to be single.

■ Talk to people: a married couple, a religious brother or sister, a deacon, priest, bishop, or a single person.

■ Value the unique person God created you as: your personality, your gifts, your talents. Think about the best way you can use your gifts and talents to live a holy life.

Remember that discernment is an ongoing process. The more time you give to it, the better you will become at discovering who God is calling you to be.

MY FAITH CHOICE

This week I will set aside time to discern God's calling for me. I will:

_____

_____

_____.

 PRAY Lord of life, by my Baptism you have called me to serve the Church in her work. Help me to continually embrace your call to holiness so that I may be generous with your Word. Amen.

Recall

Define each of these faith vocabulary terms:

1. charism _____

2. consecrated life _____

3. laity _____

4. ordained ministry _____

Choose one of the questions below and write a brief paragraph to answer your choice.

5. Describe the Church as the People of God.

_____

_____

6. Describe the role of the laity in the Church.

_____

_____

Reflect

Using what you have learned in this chapter, reflect on and describe in your own words the meaning of this statement:

> [T]he Church, being the salt of the earth and the light of the world, is more urgently called upon to save and renew every [person], that all things may be restored in Christ, and all [people] may constitute one family in Him and one people of God. AD GENTES [ON THE MISSION ACTIVITY OF THE CHURCH], 1

_____

_____

Share

With a partner, describe the role of the ordained ministers in the Church.

WITH MY FAMILY

Discuss how your family can be a sign to others that God calls all people to be one family, the People of God.

To Help You REMEMBER

1. The Church is the sacrament of God's love for the whole world.

2. The Church is a pilgrim people called together by God to become one in Jesus Christ.

3. There are four states of life: single, married, consecrated, and ordained.

Prayer for VOCATIONS

Leader: God the Father calls each member of the Church to share in and continue the work of his Son. Let us listen to the Word of God.

Reader 1: A reading from the first Letter of Paul to the Corinthians. (*Proclaim 1 Corinthians 12:27–31.*)

The word of the Lord.

All: **Thanks be to God.**

Leader: Take a few moments to think about your gifts and talents. Ask yourself how God is calling you to use these blessings. (Pause.)

Lord God, we ask that we may know and follow the vocation to which you are calling us.

All: **Lord, hear our prayer.**

Reader 2: We pray for those who serve your people as bishops, priests, and deacons.

All: **Lord, hear our prayer.**

Reader 3: We pray for consecrated religious and for those who serve your people as single people.

All: **Lord, hear our prayer.**

Reader 4: We pray for those who serve you as Christian married spouses and for their families.

All: **Lord, hear our prayer.**

Leader: Lord God, Father of all, send faith-filled workers to continue the work of Christ, your Son. Send the Holy Spirit to be their helper and guide. We ask this through Christ our Lord.

All: **Amen.**

LOOKING AHEAD
In this chapter the Holy Spirit invites you to ▶

EXPLORE how Saint Bridget served the Church.
DISCOVER why the Church is the Body of Christ.
DECIDE on how you can help build up the Body of Christ.

CHAPTER **3**

THE MYSTERY OF THE CHURCH

▶ Which things in life are a mystery to you?

Some situations are problems to be solved. And others seem beyond our understanding. We often look at these kinds of situations as mysteries.

The Church is a mystery, a mystery that only faith can accept. The Church is made up of both human and divine components. That is, the Church has both visible and spiritual aspects.

[There is] one Lord, one faith, one baptism, one God and Father of all, who is over all and through all and in all.

EPHESIANS 4:5–6

▶ How do you see the Church as mystery?

TIMELINE

1075–1211 Cathedral of Santiago de Compostela	**1303–1373** Life of St. Bridget of Sweden		**1993** *Veritatis Splendor* reinforces common good.

1050	1300	1900	1950	2000

| | **1928** Invention of sliced bread machine | **1945** Establishment of the United Nations | |

A Visionary WOMAN

Bridget of Sweden

All disciples of the Risen Christ are called to be his hands and feet and heart. Each of us is called to witness to Jesus' love in the world. As Saint Paul says,

As a body is one though it has many parts, and all the parts of the Body, though many, are one body, so also is Christ ." 1 CORINTHIANS 12:12

Some of us are called by God to be like the prophets of ancient Israel. We are to boldly speak out against the sins of the world. Others are mystics who have very powerful experiences of God's presence. Some Christians see wonderful visions in which Christ, Mary, and the Saints appear in heavenly glory and offer comforting messages. These Christian prophets are commonly called visionaries. Many of them have been women.

Saint Bridget of Sweden was one of the leading visionaries of her time. She was born around 1303 into wealth and nobility. As a young teen, Bridget married a man of Swedish royalty. They went on to have eight children (one of their daughters, Catherine of Sweden, is also a Saint.) Bridget's family members took their faith seriously. For many generations, her male ancestors made the long and dangerous pilgrimage to the Holy Land. They went to see the places where Jesus had lived and died.

▶ **What is one of the most powerful experiences of prayer that you have had?**

A Pilgrimage for Christ

Bridget herself was a pilgrim for most of her life. Around 1344, she and her husband made the long pilgrimage to the Cathedral of Santiago de Compostela in Spain. On the way home, Bridget's husband fell sick. He died shortly after they returned to Sweden. Bridget wondered what she would do once she was widowed. Then she had a vision that determined her actions for the rest of her life. She heard Jesus call her his "bride" and his "channel." She would be a channel of communication through which Jesus would make his will known to those around her.

Sometimes when we take a stand for Jesus, others might not understand. Bridget's prayerfulness and courage, however, gave her the confidence to trust Jesus' words.

Blessed are you when they insult you and persecute you and utter every kind of evil against you (falsely) because of me. Rejoice and be glad for your reward will be great in heaven.

MATTHEW 5:11–12

Bridget was deeply troubled by the wickedness of the royal court in Sweden. She fearlessly condemned its sins. In response, the lords and ladies of the court ridiculed Bridget. One lord whose evil conduct Bridget had criticized poured a bucket of dirty water on her head as she walked down the street.

Disheartened by the immorality of the court, Bridget made a pilgrimage to Rome during the 1350 Holy Year. Rather than return to Sweden, she spent the last thirty years of her life generously helping poor pilgrims in Italy. When she was sixty-nine, Bridget had some of her most famous visions while on a pilgrimage to the Holy Land. She died the following year.

Bridget's reputation for holiness was so great that she was declared a Saint in 1391, only eighteen years after her death. Her feast day is July 23.

Cathedral of Santiago de Compostela, Spain

FAITH JOURNAL

Explain how you understand the connection between praying and living as a disciple of Jesus.

_____

_____

_____

_____

_____

_____

_____

_____

_____

The Beauty of Mystery

We believe in many mysteries of faith. A **mystery of faith** is something we believe because of what God has revealed and what the Church teaches. The truths of faith can never be fully understood. There will always be more that we can learn and understand. This is the beauty of the mysteries of faith.

One reason the Church is a mystery is that the Church is made up of both a visible, or earthly, reality and an invisible, or spiritual, reality. The Church is both a human community with a hierarchical structure and a spiritual communion that mirrors the unity of the Holy Trinity. The Church is both an earthly reality that exists here and now, and a reality that exists in Heaven, where the Lord reigns in glory surrounded by Mary and all the Saints.

From the days of the early Church, Christians have used images to describe the nature and work of the Church. These images can only tell us a partial truth about the mystery of the Church.

▶ What is one symbol that helps you understand the mystery of the Trinity?

The NATURE of the CHURCH

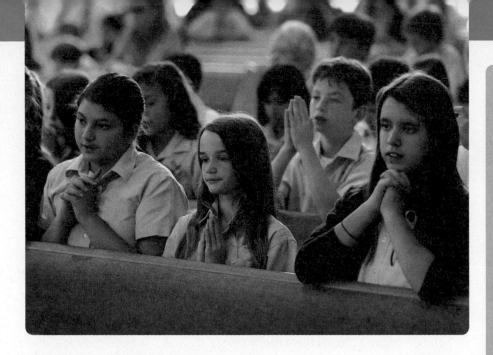

Images of Church

If the Church is Mystery, then we can never fully define what she is or fully understand the movement of the Holy Spirit within the Church. To help us gain some insight into the mystery of the Church, the Church offers us three important images: the Body of Christ, the Temple of the Holy Spirit, and the Sacrament of Salvation.

The Body of Christ

The image of the Body of Christ compares the Church to the functioning of the human body. Saint Paul writes:

> *Now you are Christ's body, and individually parts of it.*
>
> 1 CORINTHIANS 12:27

As the parts of a physical body are united one to another, so too Christians are united with one another in Christ. Christ is "the head of the body, the church" (Colossians 1:18). Christ directs and gives life to us. Together we make up the "whole Christ."

Paul reminds us that living as members of the Body of Christ means that we respect the unique gifts and charisms of others because we know that the Holy Spirit has given these gifts for the sake of the entire Church and the world. Each one of us must also recognize our own unique gifts and charisms, develop them, and place them at the service of the Church and of the world.

If we think about Paul's image of the Church as the Body of Christ, we will also come to understand something wonderful. If we are the Body of Christ, then we are to be the hands and the feet and the heart of Jesus in our world today! Just as Jesus taught and showed God's love to those he met during his earthly life, so the Risen Christ continues his ministry through us.

Catholics BELIEVE

One of the most fascinating terms used by the Vatican II Council was the phrase, "the Mystical Body of Christ." This term refers to all of those women and men, past, present and future, who are united in an eternal relationship with the Risen Christ and with one another. This Mystical Body of Christ, so called because we cannot ever know the full size and shape of it, "subsists" in the visible Roman Catholic Church.

Faith CONNECTION

Identify ways in which you can be the hands, feet, and heart of Christ to others.

Bread from Heaven

Reflecting upon the Church as the Body of Christ, we are reminded of another way we experience Christ's Body as the Church. The Evangelists included bread and meal stories in their accounts of the Gospel to remind us that Jesus is the Bread come down from Heaven. When we eat this bread at our celebration of the Eucharist each Sunday, we are receiving Jesus' Body into our own.

One time Jesus had been teaching and curing people. Getting into a boat with his disciples, Jesus crossed the Sea of Tiberias, also called the Sea of Galilee. Mark the Evangelist tells us what happened next:

When he (Jesus) disembarked and saw the vast crowd, his heart was moved with pity for them, for they were like sheep without a shepherd; and he began to teach them many things. By now it was already late and his disciples approached him and said, "This is a deserted place and it is already very late. Dismiss them so that they can go to the surrounding farms and villages and buy themselves something to eat." He said to them in reply, "Give them some food yourselves...." So he gave orders to have them sit down in groups on the green grass. The people took their places in rows by hundreds and by fifties. Then, taking the five loaves and the two fish and looking up to heaven, he said the blessing, broke the loaves, and gave them to [his] disciples to set before the people; he also divided the two fish among them all. They all ate and were satisfied.

MARK 6:34–37, 39–42

Christians have come to understand that this Gospel passage connects to our celebration of the Eucharist and also points to the future life in God's kingdom. We see this more closely when we also read Jesus' teaching in John 6:22–71. In this teaching, which is called "The Bread of Life Discourse," Jesus says:

> *"I am the bread of life. Your ancestors ate the manna in the desert, but they died; this is the bread that comes down from heaven so that one may eat it and not die."*
> JOHN 6:48–50

▶ **Why is mealtime important for families to spend together?**

Temple of the Holy Spirit

The image of the Church as the Temple of the Holy Spirit is used to describe the indwelling of the Holy Spirit in the Church and within the hearts of the faithful. Saint Paul used this image in his first Letter to the Corinthians: "Do you not know that you are the temple of God, and that the Spirit of God dwells in you" (1 Corinthians 3:16). The Holy Spirit is the source of the richness of the Church's charisms (see 1 Corinthians 12:27–31). Recall that charisms are special graces given to individuals by the Holy Spirit to be used "so that the church may be built up" (1 Corinthians 14:5).

For Paul and the rest of the first generation of Christians, this image had a specific and important meaning. The Jewish people believed that God dwells in the Temple in Jerusalem, specifically, the innermost room of the Temple, known as the "Holy of Holies." This was why every Jew who could do so was expected to make a pilgrimage to the Temple, where they were to offer sacrifice and pray.

When Paul says that the Church is the Temple of God, he is saying that the fullness of God dwells within the Church. The Church, as the Body of Christ, is the New Temple, one in which the Holy Spirit dwells. In the Church, we encounter the Risen Lord, God himself.

> *"For where two or three are gathered together in my name, there am I in the midst of them."*
> MATTHEW 18:20

Chapel tabernacle, Mafra Basillica, Portugal

Faith CONNECTION

Which actions during the Mass help you to experience the presence of God?

Sacrament of Salvation

The Church teaches that she is "the universal sacrament of salvation" and the "visible plan of God's love for humanity" (CCC 776). To understand the beauty of this image, reflect on what the Church teaches about what a sacrament is. A **sacrament** is an outward sign instituted by Christ and entrusted to the Church to give grace. Sacraments are the visible, physical, and sensory signs that help us connect to the invisible, spiritual, and mysterious reality of God.

The Church as a sacrament means that the faithful are the visible sign of God in the world. We as the Body of Christ can help others connect with God. And the Church herself, because of the indwelling Holy Spirit guiding her, is entrusted to sanctify the world for the sake of Salvation.

This sign of the Church as sacrament is however only an instrument. Therefore the Church is not God, but God's instrument in the world to do his will. So the Church points all of us in a real and specific way to the presence of God working in our lives and in our world.

This is an awesome mystery and a great responsibility that we all hold as Jesus' disciple. Each of us as faithful members of the Church is to be "salt of the earth" and a "light in the world" (see Matthew 5:13-16). We, as the one Body of Christ, are to love as God loves, unconditionally and with sacrifice.

Faith CONNECTION

How have you helped others experience God's unconditional love?

_____

_____

_____

_____

_____

_____

_____

_____

BELONGING to Groups

We all have a basic need to belong. Humans were not made to live in isolation; we need other people. Yes, there are times when we choose to be alone, but we all like to belong to groups where we are accepted, have fun, and work together.

We all belong to the Family of God. Through Baptism you have the wonderful gift of being joined to Christ and belonging to the Church, the Body of Christ. Throughout your life you will belong to many other groups. Your own families, classes in school, teams, clubs, and organizations are only a few examples. Members of a group share together, learn to trust each other, recognize one another's gifts and talents, and learn how to work together.

Sometimes working in a group is a challenge. To be a vibrant, contributing member of any group you have to learn how to get along and work together for the common good.

KEYS TO CONTRIBUTE

Here are some suggestions to help you be a responsible and valued member of any group:

- Value being a member of the group through a spirit of cooperation and enthusiasm.

- Express your opinions honestly while being respectful of other members and their ideas.

- Participate in various activities of the group, especially in the planning of events by offering solutions.

- Work cooperatively for the good of the group, being sure that you meet your responsibilities.

  - Ask God's blessings on the group and pray for his help in accomplishing the goals of the group.

    Describe how you have experienced a group's success.

    _____

    _____

    _____

MY FAITH CHOICE

This week I will contribute to the work of my school or parish by:

_____

_____.

 PRAY Most Holy Trinity, help me to love as you love, being a gift to others according to their needs. Amen.

Recall

Define each of these faith vocabulary terms:

1. Body of Christ _____

2. Holy of Holies _____

3. mystery of faith _____

4. sacrament _____

Choose one of the questions below and write a brief paragraph to respond.

5. Read Luke 9:10–17 (Feeding of the Five Thousand). Explain how this Gospel account is an image of the Church.

_____

_____

6. Discuss what it means to say that the Church is Mystery.

_____

_____

To Help You REMEMBER

1. The Church is Mystery, a communion of God and humanity; both visible and invisible.

2. We are the Body of Christ, who are called to be the hands, feet, and heart of Christ to others.

3. God is fully present within the Church, through the Holy Spirit.

Reflect

Using what you have learned in this chapter, reflect on and describe in your own words the meaning of this statement:

Through [Christ] the whole structure is held together and grows into a temple sacred in the Lord; in him you also are being built together into a dwelling place of God in the Spirit. EPHESIANS 2:21–22

_____

_____

Share

Name specific ways in which you can be the hands, feet and heart of Christ for others.

WITH MY FAMILY

Discuss with your family: How is our family a sign that the Church is the Body of Christ?

Prayer for
GOD'S PEOPLE

Leader: Praying for others is one way we show our caring love for them. Let us pray for people in need so that they may come to know and trust in God's caring presence among them. Lord God, Father of all, look lovingly on your people.

Reader: Bless your Church with the spirit of generosity and mercy so she may serve all those in need. We pray:

All: **Lord, hear us.**

Reader: Bless our nation with the spirit of compassion and kindness to reach out and share her blessings with the poorest among us. We pray:

All: **Lord, hear us.**

Reader: Bless people who are suffering spiritually and physically with the strength of your healing love. We pray:

All: **Lord, hear us.**

Reader: Bless people who are hungry and are in need of shelter with the gift of people who share their blessings with them. We pray:

All: **Lord, hear us.**

Reader: Bless (all privately add their personal petitions). We pray:

All: **Lord, hear us.**

Leader: God our Father,
in Jesus Christ, your Son,
your caring love for us was most fully revealed.
May we always trust in that love.

All: **Amen.**

LOOKING AHEAD
In this chapter the Holy Spirit invites you to ▶

EXPLORE ways we serve our communities.
DISCOVER the meaning of the Four Marks of the Church.
DECIDE how you can share your unique gifts with others.

CHAPTER **4**

The Marks of the Church

▶ **Which qualities or characteristics make you unique?**

God created each of us unique in his image and likeness. You have particular abilities, perhaps a gift for sports, music, the arts, or learning. Maybe you are a good listener and so your friends trust you.

Just as each of us has certain qualities that make us unique, so too the Church has specific characteristics that make her unique.

But you are "a chosen race, a royal priesthood, a holy nation, a people of his own, so that you may announce the praises" of him who called you out of darkness into his wonderful light.

1 PETER 2:9

▶ **Which characteristics of the Church first come to mind?**

TIMELINE

		1950 Infallibility of Mary's Assumption declared.	1964 Vatican II's *Decree on Ecumenism*		2001 Establishment of the USCCB	
1900	1920	1940	1960	1980	2000	2010

1917
US entry into WWI

1950
National Council of Churches in US is formed.

45

Local Ministry

The Bishops in the U.S.

The apostolic nature of our Church is clearly seen in the ministry of the bishops, who are the spiritual descendants of the Twelve Apostles. Together with the Pope and under his authority they share in the responsibility and mission Jesus entrusted to the Apostles.

Bishops throughout the world proclaim the Gospel and remind us to live according to God's Law. In the United States, the bishops do this together through the United States Conference of Catholic Bishops (USCCB). The USCCB is the assembly of bishops who guide Catholics in the U.S. to live the Gospel.

The creation of a council of U.S. bishops started during World War I. Under the leadership of James Cardinal Gibbons of Baltimore, the National Catholic War Council was formed. This council demonstrated the value of the national collaboration of bishops. In a 1919 letter, Pope Benedict XV urged the U.S. hierarchy to join him in working for peace and social justice. The bishops responded by deciding to meet annually. After the Second Vatican Council, the U.S. bishops continued the work begun in 1917. By 2001 a single organization, the United States Conference of Catholic Bishops, was formed.

▶ Which issue would you want the U.S. bishops to focus most on?

Parish Ministry

Community is a clear sign of the great integrity with which the Church lives out the mark of holiness. For example, the H.U.G.S. (Hearts United Giving & Sharing) Truck ministry of Saint Mark the Evangelist Catholic Church shows its solidarity with the poor on a regular basis.

Each month the people of Saint Mark Catholic Church collect canned food, gently-used clothing and furniture, and other everyday items like soap, shampoo, and school supplies. The collection takes place after each Mass on an assigned Sunday. The collected goods are loaded onto a truck and transported to the sister parish where people in need can receive the items.

Saint Mark's H.U.G.S. Truck ministry represents a massive effort to help others. The spiritual dimension of this ministry consists of reflecting on how to use one's time and talents to best live the Gospel and serve the Kingdom of God.

In extending themselves in service to their poorer sisters and brothers, the people of Saint Mark's offer a living example of what holiness looks like. They recognize that no matter what our economic differences might be, all of God's people are one.

FAITH JOURNAL

What are some other examples of serving the needy? How can you become involved in helping other people?

_____

_____

_____

_____

_____

_____

_____

_____

_____

► FAITH FOCUS

What are the Four Marks of the Church?

─────────────

► FAITH VOCABULARY

apostolic succession

ecumenism

infallibility

Magisterium

I Believe

At Sunday Mass we pray the Nicene Creed or Apostles' Creed. Each of us professes, "I believe in one, holy, catholic, and apostolic Church." One, holy, catholic, and apostolic are the Four Marks of the Church. These marks are the essential characteristics of the Church founded by Jesus Christ. These four marks help us understand the mystery and mission of the Church.

The Church Is One

Christ founded only one Church. The visible bonds that unite Christ's followers as one Church include:

1. the profession of one faith received from the Apostles

2. a common worship, especially Baptism, the Eucharist, and the other Sacraments

3. direct succession of bishops from the Apostles through the Sacrament of Holy Orders

These bonds of unity are found most fully in the Catholic Church. Christians who do not share fully with the Catholic Church are joined to us "in some, although imperfect, communion" (*Decree on Ecumenism* 3). In those Churches and communities who are not in full communion with the Catholic Church, there are elements of holiness and truth that are truly means of Salvation.

Scripture reveals to us that Jesus founded one Church. Just prior to being arrested, Jesus prayed:

[S]o that they may all be one, as you, Father, are in me and I in you, that they also may be in us, that the world may believe that you sent me.

JOHN 17:21

All Christians must make Jesus' prayer their own prayer. We must pray and work for the restoration of the unity of the Church. God calls us to be united in the Church as the Father, Son, and Holy Spirit are united. We call this work of the Church **ecumenism**.

The Universal Church

▶ Identify ways in which you demonstrate your unity with other Christians.

The Church Is Holy

The Church is holy because the Holy Spirit dwells within and guides the Church. In Baptism we are joined to Christ, become adopted children of God the Father, and receive the gift of the Holy Spirit. All baptized Christians share in the life and love of God, the Holy One. Each of us receives the grace to live a life of holiness through the actions of the Church.

Through his Death and Resurrection, Christ has won forgiveness of sins and reconciliation with God for the entire human race. Jesus is "the way and the truth and the life" in whom Salvation is found (John 14:6). In this sense the Church teaches that all Salvation—even the Salvation of the unbaptized—comes from Christ through his Body, the Church.

The Church Is Catholic

The word *catholic* means "universal." This Mark of the Church tells us that in God's plan all people are to become the one People of God. The Church of Christ that we profess in the Creed is found fully in the Catholic Church.

The catholic nature of the Church is demonstrated by the diversity within the Church. The Roman Catholic Church is in communion with a number of Eastern Catholic Churches. The Churches in the West and in the East are often grouped according to the rites they celebrate and the cultural or ethnic faith traditions they share in common. A rite is the "liturgical, theological, spiritual and disciplinary patrimony, culture and circumstances of history of a distinct people, by which its own manner of living the faith is manifested" (*Code of Canons of the Eastern Catholic Churches* 1990).

The Eastern Catholic Churches are in full communion with the Catholic Church, yet some Greek and Russian Churches are not. These Churches have their origins in the Middle East, the cradle of the Christian Church. For example, the Alexandrian Church traces her roots to the desert traditions of Egypt. While the Alexandrian Church recognizes the bishop of Rome, the Pope, as the leader of the Universal Church, they are governed by a patriarch.

These Eastern Churches all celebrate a common faith with the Catholic Church, according to traditions and rites influenced by the ancient cultures around Jerusalem, Antioch, Alexandria, and Constantinople.

The Church is Apostolic

Apostolic means "from the time of the Apostles." The Church has her origin and foundation in the life of the Twelve Apostles whom Jesus chose to act in his name. Ever since that time, leadership in the Church has been handed down from Saint Peter and the other Apostles to the Popes and bishops through the Sacrament of Holy Orders. This connection of all Popes and bishops back to Saint Peter and the first Apostles is called **apostolic succession**.

Apostolic succession is essential to the faith of the Catholic Church. Even the canon of the New Testament was formed according to the books' connections to one of the Apostles. Saint John the Apostle and Evangelist says this clearly:

> It is this disciple who testifies to these things and has written them, and we know that his testimony is true.
>
> JOHN 21:24.

All of Sacred Scripture has been faithfully handed down to us according to the testimony of these first witnesses. So in like manner, the laying on of hands during the ordination of a bishop sacramentally transmits the ecclesial authority given by Jesus to the Apostles down through all the bishops of the Catholic Church.

▶ **How can you testify to the truth that Christ has given to the Church?**

DID YOU KNOW?

Since the days of the early Church, the Apostles and their successors have written letters to teach and guide the Church. This tradition still exists today. The writing of pastoral letters is one way the bishops of the United States, either individually or together as the United States Conference of Catholic Bishops (USCCB), instruct the faithful on Catholic teachings, worship, social concerns, and other topics that are important to the life of the Church.

The Church as Teacher

Jesus made Saint Peter the "rock," or visible foundation, on which he would build the Church (see Matthew 16:18–19). Peter and his successors would be the visible sign of unity for the Church founded by Jesus. The successors of Saint Peter (Popes) and the Apostles (bishops) are the teaching authority of the Church, guided by the Holy Spirit. This living teaching authority of the Church, entrusted to the Pope and the bishops by Christ, is called the **Magisterium**.

The Church uses the term College of Bishops to name the unity of all the bishops and the special leadership, or primacy, of the Pope among the bishops. The Pope as the successor of Saint Peter and head of the College of Bishops has a special authority in the Church. He has "supreme, full, immediate, and universal authority over the care of souls by divine institution" (*Christus Dominus* 2). When the Pope and the bishops act together in their capacity as the College of Bishops, they exercise supreme and full teaching authority over the universal Church. The Church refers to this as **infallibility**.

This infallibility teaching is the charism of the Holy Spirit given to the Church that guarantees that the official teaching of the Pope or the Pope and bishops on matters of faith and morals is without error. This charism is at work when:

1. the Pope teaches officially as the supreme pastor of the Church, or

2. the College of Bishops teaches together with the Pope.

The Catholic faithful are required to accept such teachings with the obedience of faith.

Faith CONNECTION

What are some questions you would like to ask your pastor about the teaching of the Church?

Build Up the Church

While only bishops participate in apostolic succession, all the baptized are called to work together to build up the Church. One way we do this work is through parish councils. A parish council is made up of members of the parish family. These representatives are either appointed by the pastor or elected by parishioners and approved by the pastor.

Parish councils help the pastor with his managerial and pastoral tasks. This council fosters a sense of community by developing and promoting programs that touch the lives of the members of the parish. They also help the parish reach out to the members of the wider community. Parish councils are often organized into dynamic committees. Examples of these committees include finance, administration, education, social justice, spiritual development, ecumenism, evangelism, and parish activities.

A parish community contains a whole host of people who use their talents and skills to build up the Church and take part in her mission. For example, parishioners who are social workers, artists, nurses, skilled laborers, merchants, business leaders, secretaries, lawyers, doctors, educators, and so on, can use their gifts to help create vibrant faith communities.

Among the issues that councils tackle are the continuing need for parish volunteers, youth education, development and implementation of parish mission statements, caring for the needy, adult education, and the challenges to serve a growing Catholic population.

Faith CONNECTION

How does your parish or school touch the lives of the community?

SHARING Resources

Jesus taught that all his disciples are to share their blessings with others. Whether we are wealthy or poor, Jesus asks us to share our resources, especially with those in need.

The truth is, whether you have a lot of material things or hardly any at all, you do have certain gifts and talents that you are called to share with others. If we all share whatever resources we have, we all benefit. As a disciple of Jesus, you can help others come to know God's great love and care for them. You can come to know more deeply God's love and goodness in your own life.

SHARING GIFTS

Part of being a person of integrity involves using the unique talents and gifts God has given you for the needs of others.

Here are examples of some gifts and talents that you may have, which you can generously share with others:

- intelligence—by tutoring someone who needs help in a certain subject

- time—by listening and helping someone who needs a friend

- singing or dancing—by entertaining someone, or cheering them up

- playing sports—by helping coach younger children

- cooking—by helping your family prepare meals

In a small group, discuss why it is better to give than to receive.

MY FAITH CHOICE

This week I can show that I am a person of integrity by sharing my unique gifts and talents for the sake or need of another. I will:

_____

_____

 PRAY Heavenly Father, you have blessed all of creation with so much. Help me to appreciate the gifts you have given me by sharing them with others. Amen.

Recall

Define each of these faith vocabulary terms:

1. apostolic succession _____

2. ecumenism _____

3. infallibility _____

4. Magisterium _____

Choose one of the questions below and write a brief paragraph to answer your choice.

5. Explain how the Four Marks of the Church help us understand the mystery of the Church.

_____

_____

6. Explain how the work of the Magisterium helps us live as faithful and responsible members of the Church.

_____

_____

To Help You REMEMBER

1. The Four Marks of the Church are traits that make the Church unique.

2. The Catholic Church works for unity among all peoples, especially among Christians.

3. The Magisterium is the teaching authority of the Church.

Reflect

Using what you have learned in this chapter, reflect on and describe in your own words the meaning of this statement:

Whatever is truly Christian is never contrary to what genuinely belongs to the faith; indeed, it can always bring a deeper realization of the mystery of Christ and the Church. DECREE ON ECUMENISM (UNITATIS REDINTEGRATIO) 4

_____

_____

Share

Discuss with a partner how integrity is important to building up the Church.

WITH MY FAMILY

Discuss with your family: How else can we become more involved in the life of our parish?

Happy in Your House

Leader: O Lord, happy are those who trust in you.

All: Happy are those who live in your House, singing praise to you.

Group 1: I long to be in your Temple,

Group 2: Even sparrows have built nests near your altars.

All: Happy are those who live in your House, singing praise to you.

Group 1: One day spent in your Temple is better than one thousand spent elsewhere.

Group 2: I would rather be a doorkeeper at your Temple than live in the homes of the wicked.

All: Happy are those who live in your House, singing praise to you.

Group 1: The Lord is our protector, blessing us with love and honor.

Group 2: The Lord does not withhold anything from those who do right.

All: Happy are those who live in your House, singing praise to you.

BASED ON PSALM 84

Leader: Lord God, you call us to be your Church. May we always be aware that we live in your presence, one God who is Father, Son, and Holy Spirit.

All: Amen.

LOOKING AHEAD
In this chapter the Holy Spirit invites you to ▶

EXPLORE some popular Catholic devotional prayers.
DISCOVER the various kinds of prayers.
DECIDE on how to deepen your prayer life.

CHAPTER **5**

People of PRAYER

▶ **How is technology changing the way people communicate today?**

Prayer is a way we can communicate with God. Today we can use various electronic devices to aid us in our prayer life. When we pray, we raise our minds and hearts to God. We become more aware of the Risen Christ and the movement of the Holy Spirit.

It is good to give thanks to the LORD.   PSALM 92:2

▶ **What were the first prayers you learned?**

TIMELINE

	1170–1221 Life of St. Dominic de Guzmán		1542–1591 Life of St John of the Cross			1854 Immaculate Conception declared Infallible.
1100	1300	1500	1700	1800		1900

1732–1809 Life of Hayden   1756–1791 Life of Mozart

Music for the Soul

Throughout the history of the Church, many forms of prayer have developed. There are ways of praying to match everyone's needs. Many prayers have been approved by the Church and embraced by all of the faithful. Sacred music is a form of prayer through which Christians express their faith.

Hymns and Chant

The Gospel tells us that Jesus and his disciples sang at the Last Supper: "Then, after singing a hymn, they went out to the Mount of Olives" (Matthew 26:30). Singing continues to be an integral part of Christian worship and prayer life today.

Christians also express their faith through hymns. Some of the hymns that we sing today have lyrics that are based in early Church writings. Recently, Gregorian chant has become popular again. This simple yet melodic form of music was developed in the 6th century, and is named after Pope Saint Gregory the Great.

Classical Music

Around 1750 sacred music in the West reached new heights with the Austrian composers Wolfgang Amadeus Mozart (1756–1791) and Franz Joseph Haydn (1732–1809). The sacred music that they composed blended text, music, and belief in God, while others composed music without lyrics for silent prayer.

Music is more than just something in the background to set a mood. Music invites people to participate actively in the liturgy. Music helps us lift our minds and hearts to God. Music helps bind the faithful together in a communal act of worship.

▶ How does your favorite music help you praise God?

Devoted like Mary

Examples such as Mary's hymn of praise, the Magnificat, continue to inspire followers of Christ to express their prayers to God through music (see Ephesians 5:19–20). Christians celebrate and express the depth of their faith-filled love for God in ways they cannot express through words alone. Some prayers involve repeated actions involving rituals called devotions.

The Church has always recognized Mary's essential role in God's plan of Salvation. Because of her importance, there are many devotions focused on Mary that have developed within the Church.

In the early centuries of Church history, Mary was proclaimed as "theotokos" – the bearer of God and mother of Jesus. When Pope Pius IX infallibly defined the doctrine of the Immaculate Conception in 1854, he stated as divinely revealed what the Church believed—that Mary was conceived free from Original Sin.

One of the most enduring and popular devotions is the recitation of the Rosary. Although Saint Dominic is credited with introducing the Rosary to the faithful in the 13th century, Church historians believe the origins of the prayer go back much further – possibly to the rise of monasticism in the 4th century.

The Rosary continued to develop when Pope John Paul II introduced another set of mysteries called the Luminous Mysteries. The Rosary invites the faithful to reflect with Mary on the great mysteries of Salvation.

Madonna of the Magnificat by Sandro Botticelli (1445-1510)

FAITH JOURNAL

Identify how the Mysteries of the Rosary have affected your faith.

Spiritual LIFE

One Voice

The Church is a communication community. We are the People of God, joined together as the one Body of Christ, constantly communicating with God through prayer. We raise our voices as one in adoration, blessing, thanksgiving, intercession, petition, and praise of God.

All of these practices are forms of prayer, the intentional raising up of our hearts and minds to God. To pray is to recognize the presence of God in our lives, and to respond to his presence. We do this both individually and communally.

The Holy Spirit, the Third Person of the Holy Trinity, continuously invites and teaches the Church to pray. The Holy Spirit helps us remember the prayer of Abraham and Moses, Ruth and Esther, and the prayer of all the people of the Old Covenant. The same Holy Spirit recalls to our memory the prayer of Mary, Peter, and the other disciples. Most of all, the Holy Spirit reminds us of what Jesus said and taught about prayer:

> *For those who are led by the Spirit of God are children of God. . . . [Y]ou received a spirit of adoption, through which we cry, "Abba, Father!" . . . In the same way, the Spirit too comes to the aid of our weakness; for we do not know how to pray as we ought, but the Spirit itself intercedes with inexpressible groanings.*
>
> ROMANS 8:14–15, 26.

► **Describe a time when you were comforted beyond words.**

DID YOU KNOW?

In his youth, Saint Bernard of Clairvaux (1090–1153) enjoyed being alone. When he learned about a newly formed Benedictine monastery, he asked to become a member. Bernard's dedication to the prayer and work of the monastery led others to ask him to establish a new monastery that eventually became the center of sixty-eight other monasteries. The work of this quiet, shy boy, which renewed the prayer life of the Church, is still being felt in the Church today. The Church celebrates the feast day of Saint Bernard of Clairvaux, Doctor of the Church, on August 20.

Rhythm of the Church

Sacred Scripture is the Word of God. Through reading and listening to the Word of God, we encounter him speaking to us, and we listen to him. We deepen our love for God and respond to that divine love.

The prayer of the Church has a certain rhythm. This rhythm is made up of fixed times and seasons that we can mark off with regularity to ensure that the time we spend in prayer flows throughout our lives. These times and seasons include the weekly cycle of prayer centered on the Sunday Eucharist, the cycle of feasts of the Lord and of the Saints, and the seasons of the liturgical year.

There are also daily rhythms to the Church's life of prayer, such as morning and evening prayer, grace before and after meals, and the Liturgy of the Hours.

The simplest, yet very powerful, prayer that we can utter is to speak the name Jesus over and over again. This reminds us that every good grace that comes from God the Father comes through Jesus, our Lord and Savior. Jesus is present with his Church in the celebration of the Sacraments and other liturgical celebrations.

Having a regular rhythm to our prayer, like having a regular rhythm to our breathing, reenergizes our spiritual life. Prayer is our encounter with God who is always with us. Prayer strengthens our relationship with the Holy Trinity and with all the members of the Body of Christ. Prayer draws us closer to the love of God, transforms the way we think and act.

Faith CONNECTION

"He who sings (in praise to God) prays twice" is a saying attributed to Saint Augustine of Hippo. What do you think he meant?

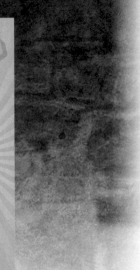

Like Mary

The stories about Mary in the Gospels show us the different ways that the Mother of Jesus prayed. In her response to the angel Gabriel, Mary models the surrender to God that is the essence of prayer (read Luke 1: 26-38). The Magnficat is a prayer of praise and adoration (read Luke 1:46-58). In the story of the Wedding of Cana, Mary approaches her son with a prayer of petition (read John 2:1-12). Standing by the Cross, Mary enters a wordless contemplation incorporating both her overwhelming grief and trust in God (Jn 19:26).

As Mary did, so we too express ourselves in many different ways through prayer. There are, however, three basic ways Christians express themselves in prayer. These expressions of prayer are **vocal prayer**, **meditation**, and **contemplation**.

Vocal Prayer

Vocal prayer is either spoken aloud or spoken within the quiet of one's heart. The expression of prayer consists of words that communicate blessing and adoration, petition and intercession, or praise and thanksgiving to God.

Meditation

In meditation we silently express what is in our hearts and on our minds. We use our imaginations, emotions, and desires to understand and follow what the Lord is asking of us.

Contemplation

Contemplation is simply being with God. Saint Teresa of Jesus (Saint Teresa of Ávila, 1515–1582), the Spanish mystic and Doctor of the Church, describes contemplative prayer as "nothing else than a close sharing between friends; it means taking time frequently to be alone with him who we know loves us."

▶ Which form of prayer do you feel least comfortable praying? Why?

Theological Virtues

The prayer of the Body of Christ, the Church, is nourished and strengthened through Sacred Scripture, through the Sacraments and liturgy of the Church, and through the Theological Virtues of faith, hope, and love. All are God's gifts to us.

Faith. Our prayer, the surge of our hearts to God, begins out of faith. We believe God meets us and we meet him in expected and unexpected ways.

Hope. Our prayer continues out of hope. We confidently wait, knowing that God listens and responds. He does only what is best for us.

Love. Out of love God invites us to share in the communion of the life and love of the Holy Trinity—God the Father, Son, and Holy Spirit. Out of love we respond yes to his invitation.

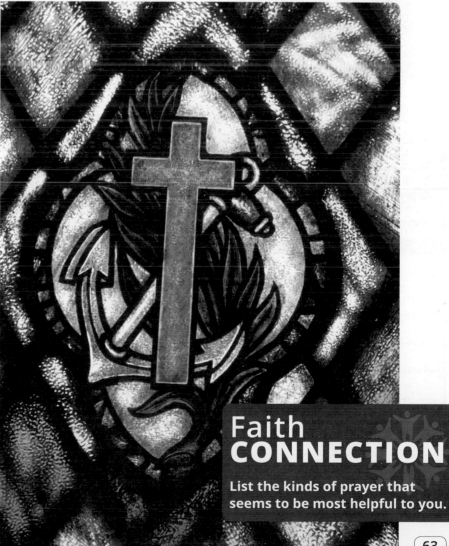

Faith CONNECTION

List the kinds of prayer that seems to be most helpful to you.

Christians do not pray only to God the Father. We pray to God the Son, Jesus Christ, and to the Father in Jesus' name. We pray to God the Holy Spirit, our helper and the Giver of life, sent to us by the Father and the Son.

However we pray, we can pray anyplace and anytime. The choice of a place to pray is important.

The Church is a favorite place for many Catholics to come for prayer throughout the day. For example, Catholics often come to visit with Christ present in the Blessed Sacrament.

Personal prayer is also essential. Our personal prayer can be enriched by setting aside a prayer corner in our homes where we can quietly read the Sacred Scripture, and listen to God's Word to us. We can also spend time with God during a walk outdoors. No matter where and when we pray, God is always there welcoming us and listening to us.

Prayer and Christian life are inseparable. Filled with the Holy Spirit we join with Jesus Christ, and with Mary and all the Saints. Together as the new People of God we offer our lives and raise our voices in praise and thanksgiving to the Father.

Faith CONNECTION

Which items would you include in your prayer space at home?

_____

_____

_____

_____

_____

_____

_____

_____

_____

Personal Prayer

Like the prayer of Jesus, the prayer of Christians is addressed primarily to God the Father. We see this in the doxologies that conclude many of the liturgical prayers of the Church. The word *doxology* means "praise-words." For example, at the conclusion of the Eucharistic Prayer we pray:

Through him, and with him, and in him, O God, almighty Father, in the unity of the Holy Spirit, all glory and honor is yours, for ever and ever. Amen.

FROM EUCHARISTIC PRAYER, ROMAN MISSAL

PRAYER of Meditation

Like the disciples who spent time with Jesus while he was on Earth, you too can spend time with Jesus. You can ask him to teach you to pray, to help you understand what it means for you to live as one of his followers. One way you can do this is through the prayer of meditation.

Taking time for meditation is a wonderful gift you can give yourself. Just taking fifteen or twenty minutes away from the noise and busyness of your day can help you relax in body and mind, and deepen your relationship with God.

PRAYER STEPS

Here are eight steps and some questions to help you get started.

- Set aside some time to meditate. What time could you set aside? Where is your quiet place to pray?

- Quiet your mind and just relax. What is the best way for you to do this?

- Pray to the Holy Spirit. Ask for help to open your mind and listen to God. If you are distracted, relax and try to refocus your thinking on God's presence in the moment.

- Choose in advance what you are going to pray about. You could focus on a poem, or a reading from Scripture.

- Begin your conversation with Jesus. What do you think Jesus would say to you?

- Use your imagination and create a scene. Picture yourself with Jesus. Where would you be? What would you talk about?

- Tell Jesus what's going on in your life right now. Ask him for what you need.

- Keep a prayer journal. Writing some reflections can be helpful in developing a prayer life.

With a partner discuss the different ways in which you pray. Discuss how you can help each other with establishing a daily habit of praying.

_____

_____

MY FAITH CHOICE

This week I will choose a time and place to pray. I will:

_____

_____.

 PRAY Lord, I adore you above all. Guide me in my relationship with you, helping me to pray without ceasing. Amen.

Recall

Define each of these faith vocabulary terms:

1. contemplation _____

2. meditation _____

3. vocal prayer _____

Choose one of the questions below and write a brief paragraph to answer your choice.

4. Cite examples for each expression of prayer (vocal prayer, meditation, contemplation).

_____

_____

5. Name and describe the sources of Christian prayer.

_____

_____

To Help You REMEMBER

1. Prayer is an essential aspect of Christian living.

2. When we pray, the Holy Spirit moves us and guides us to communicate.

3. Vocal prayer, meditation, and contemplation are the three main expressions of prayer.

Reflect

Using what you have learned in this chapter, reflect on and describe in your own words the meaning of this statement:

You don't know how to pray? Put yourself in the presence of God, and as soon as you have said, "Lord, I don't know how to pray!" you can be sure you've already begun.   Saint Josemaria Escriva

_____

_____

Share

Discuss with friends and list current songs that help you grow in your prayer life.

WITH MY FAMILY

Discuss with your family: How can we strengthen our rhythm of praying together as a family?

The MAGNIFICAT

Leader: Mary is a model of prayer for all Christians. Let us join with her in praising God.

All: "My soul proclaims the greatness of the Lord; my spirit rejoices in God my savior.

Group 1: For he has looked upon his handmaid's lowliness; behold, from now on will all ages call me blessed.

Group 2: The Mighty One has done great things for me, and holy is his name.

Group 1: His mercy is from age to age to those who fear him.

Group 2: He has shown might with his arm, dispersed the arrogant of mind and heart.

Group 1: He has thrown down the rulers from their thrones but lifted up the lowly.

Group 2: The hungry he has filled with good things; the rich he has sent away empty.

Group 1: He has helped Israel his servant, remembering his mercy,

Group 2: according to his promise to our fathers, to Abraham and to his descendants forever.

All: My soul proclaims the greatness of the Lord; my spirit rejoices in God my savior."

LUKE 1:46–55,46

LOOKING AHEAD
In this chapter the Holy Spirit invites you to ▶

EXPLORE the contributions of the monastic life.
DISCOVER the various ways the Church prays together.
DECIDE how you can pray with the Church.

CHAPTER **6**

Prayer of the CHURCH

▶ **How do you spend a typical day at home?**

Prayer is spending time with God, talking and listening to him. Our time with God is so vital that he does not wait for us to come to him. The Holy Spirit tirelessly reaches out to everyone, inviting us to prayer.

LORD, *hear my prayer; . . .*
for in you I trust. PSALM 143:1, 8

▶ **When are some of the best times of the day for you to pray?**

TIMELINE

1090–1153 Life of St. Bernard of Clairvaux	**1270** Use of Franciscan version of Divine Office		**1626–1700** Life of Jean-Armand le Bouthillier de Rancé
1000	1200	1400	1600	1800

1411 First water papermill in Portugal

1774 De-inking process invented.

Monastic LIFE

Quiet Places

Throughout the history of the Church women and men have gathered together in quiet places to be with God. Gradually, these communities formed monasteries. Those called to monastic life sometimes describe it as a means to enter more completely into the "heart of Jesus" and pray for the needs of the world.

Balanced Life

More than anyone else, the person who is credited with developing the essential principles of monastic life in the Roman Catholic Church is Saint Benedict of Nursia (480–540 AD). Benedict devoted his life to God. He founded monasteries so that he and others would have places of peace and solitude, dedicating their lives to God through prayer, work and learning.

Benedict established a monastery in Vicovaro and a larger one on Monte Cassino, also near Rome. Benedict realized that, as monastic communities became larger, he needed to develop rules so that the monastery would be "a school of the Lord's service, in which we hope to order nothing harsh or rigorous." The Rule of Saint Benedict, as it came to be known, helped those in monastic life balance work, prayer, rest and service. This rule became the standard for monastic life in the West even today.

▶ How do you balance prayer, work, rest, play, and service in your life?

Monastic Renewal

The renewal of monasticism throughout the history of the Church has contributed significantly to helping people deepen their spiritual life. In the tenth and eleventh centuries the monasteries at Cluny and Clairvaux became focal points for the renewal of monasticism, particularly for living the Rule of Saint Benedict.

Bernard of Fontaines, later known as Saint Bernard of Clairvaux, began the renewal of monasticism at Citeaux in 1112. Before he died in 1153, Bernard and his followers founded about 300 other monasteries. The Order of Cistercians (named after the site of their origin, Citeaux), continued to grow to 742 monasteries by the 1500s.

In the seventeenth century, the Cistercians themselves experienced renewal. A new order, begun under the leadership of Jean-Armand le Bouthillier de Rancé, grew out of the Cistercians and became known as the Trappists. The work of the quiet Bernard of Clairvaux still renews the twenty-first-century Church.

The essential principles of monastic life are not only practiced by those living in monasteries. The Oblates of Saint Benedict are married or single laypeople living in the world. They are dedicated to living the Rule of Saint Benedict, including the evangelical counsels of obedience, poverty, and chastity.

FAITH JOURNAL

If you were to draw up a plan for improving your prayer life, what would that plan involve?

▶ FAITH FOCUS

How is prayer vital for the Church?

▶ FAITH VOCABULARY

icons

liturgy

rites

The Heart of Prayer

Spending time with God—sharing our life with him and listening to him—is at the heart of our relationship with God. The mystery and wonder of prayer is that God always begins our conversation with him. God desires that we live in covenant with him.

The truth is that we are so connected with God that life without him is not possible. God has created us and entered into the Covenant with us. More than anything else, God wants a relationship with each and every one of us. Through Baptism we are joined to Christ, the new and everlasting Covenant. We are united in Christ with the Father and the Holy Spirit. Christian prayer is an expression of that covenantal relationship with God.

Prayer as Communion

Our prayer is a sign that our lives as children of God is alive. When we pray, we are living our relationship, or communion, with God the Father, with his Son, Jesus Christ, and with the Holy Spirit (see Ephesians 3:18–21). God desires that we live in communion with him.

Obstacles to Prayer

The truth is that communicating with God on a regular basis takes practice and requires discipline. We struggle with prayer for many reasons. Some of them are:

- We misunderstand what prayer really is.

- We become discouraged when we pray and do not see results.

- We are sometimes so busy and distracted that God cannot get a word in.

▶ What other things can be obstacles to prayer, to living in communion with God?

Models of
PRAYER

(Left) Moses, (Center) King David, (Right) Mary

People of Prayer

In Sacred Scripture, we read about people of prayer. We listen to stories of the many conversations between God and his people. We learn how they prayed and overcame the obstacles to their prayer.

We call Abraham and Sarah our parents in faith for good reason. Solely on God's promise to them, Abraham and Sarah and their family packed up all their belongings. In faith they did what God asked (see Genesis 12:4).

From that first moment of his approaching the burning bush, Moses went back and forth in conversation with God. Those face-to-face meetings with God, or moments of contemplative prayer, transformed Moses' life (see Exodus 33:11).

David, the shepherd-king of God's people, drew up plans to build a temple in which the people would gather in prayer in the presence of God (see 2 Samuel 7:18–29).

The Scriptures are also filled with many conversations that Deborah, Hannah, Isaiah, Ezekiel, Jeremiah, and other prophets had with God—conversations that refocused the attention of God's people on God and living the Covenant with him, and waiting and preparing for the promised Savior (see Isaiah 6:5, 8, 11; Jeremiah 20:7–18).

Model of Prayer

The Blessed Virgin Mary is a model of prayer for Christians. Trusting in God's promises to his people, Mary unexpectedly learned that God had chosen her to become the mother of his Son, whom she was to name Jesus.

Mary was a woman of prayer. She lived a life of faith, hope, and love. God's love for her and her love for God filled her heart in a way that no one before had ever experienced.

Faith CONNECTION

Hand write a letter to someone who is a good prayer role model for you. Thank them for helping you mature in your prayer life.

Pray like Jesus

Jesus most fully reveals the way of prayer. Jesus taught us to pray, "Our Father in heaven." He invited us to approach God the Father in prayer and trust him as "Abba," a loving Father whose most driving concern in life was the good and well-being of his children.

Throughout his life on Earth, Jesus demonstrated this kind of trust in God. Again and again, Jesus spent time alone with his Father before making important decisions. In prayer Jesus received the courage and wisdom and compassion he needed to teach, to heal, and to love all who came to him.

Jesus' whole life was a life of prayer. He lived his life on Earth in continuing conversation with his Father. He blessed and thanked his Father as the source of all blessings. He prayed for himself and for others, always confident in his Father's love for him, for his disciples, and for all people.

Life of Prayer

The whole life of the Church is a life of prayer as the life of Jesus was. Saint Paul reminds us of how vital prayer is for our lives:

Pray without ceasing. In all circumstances give thanks, for this is the will of God for you in Christ Jesus.

1 THESSALONIANS 5:17–18

Ecumenical Ceremony at Khor Virap, a monastery located in Armenia.

Christian prayer rises out of faith, out of hope, and out of love for God. Our prayer ascends in the Holy Spirit through Christ to the Father.

▶ How can a Christian's life be one of prayer?

Center of Prayer

The center of the prayer life of the Church is the **liturgy**, especially the celebration of the Eucharist. The liturgy of the Church is the worship of God. We adore God the Father as the source of all the blessings of creation and Salvation he has given us through his Son. We bless him for the gift of the Spirit through whose power we are able to call God, our Father.

Diversity of Prayer

For nearly two thousand years, the Church has developed a rich diversity of ways, or **rites**, of celebrating the liturgy. The largest number of Catholics celebrate the Latin rite. In addition to the Latin rite, there are other rites that are celebrated by Catholics around the world. Among these are those celebrated in the Byzantine, Coptic, and Chaldean Churches.

Like diversity throughout our nation, diversity in the Catholic Church is a source of enrichment. Properly recognized diversity in the celebration of the liturgy reveals the universality of the Church.

To show that we are one Church made up of many diverse liturgical traditions, we follow the guidelines that the local ordinary, the bishop of our diocese establishes. While the bishop has many other responsibilities, he is the primary liturgist in any local, or particular, church.

▶ What do you know about other rites within the Catholic Church?

Popular Devotions

In addition to the liturgy, our Christian life is nourished by a wide variety of popular devotions and piety. Popular devotions are acts of personal or communal prayer. These devotions surround and arise out of the celebration of the liturgy. They enrich and help us express and celebrate the mystery of Christian living. All of these expressions of popular piety and devotion help Christians extend the meaning of the liturgy into their homes and daily living.

Sacred Images

For centuries the Church has used sacred images, such as statues and **icons**. An icon is a picture or image of Christ, Mary, a Saint, or an angel. All sacred images used in liturgical celebrations are related to Christ. When we venerate and admire Mary, the angels, and the Saints, we do so because each of them manifests some aspect of Christ and his work of Salvation.

Christian images and other works of sacred art enable the people and events of Salvation History to become part of all cultures. They help Christians around the world remember and share in the events of the Paschal Mystery.

Faith CONNECTION

Name your favorite popular devotion or sacred work of art. How does it enrich your experience of being Catholic?

SPIRITUAL Journal

Journal writing can be a way of praying that helps you discover God's daily working in your life. Keeping a journal helps you express any special feelings you have, or describe special events of each day where you feel God's presence in your life. A spiritual journal is different from a diary— yet there are similarities. You usually write very personal things in your diary. The wonderful thing about keeping a spiritual journal is that you can share all those thoughts, feelings, fears, and joys with God.

Your spiritual journal is your dialogue with God, your personal prayer. You can also write quotes, good ideas, and thoughts from reading Scripture. You can create your own poems, prayers, or songs. You can draw pictures or paste pictures in your journal. Share with God your day.

JOURNAL STEPS

Here are a few basic steps to get you started.

- Find an appropriate book or digital device for journaling. Keep these in one special place.

- Establish a routine, a daily form of prayer, to write in your journal.

- Find a time and a place to write. Choose a place free of noise and interruption.

- Relax and pray to the Holy Spirit. Ask the Holy Spirit to enlighten your mind and open your heart.

- Date each entry. This will help you go back and find it easily.

- Write anything that comes to your mind. Use your writing as your personal dialogue with God, and listen to his response in your heart.

Decide on what are the best days, times, and places for you to write in your journal. Make a commitment here to journal about your faith.

Day: _____

Time: _____

Place: _____

MY FAITH CHOICE

This week I will commit to write in my journal about my faith. I will:

_____

_____ .

 PRAY Holy Spirit, give me the diligence to maintain a strong prayer life so that I can mature in my obedience to your will. Amen.

Recall

Define each of these faith vocabulary terms:

1. icons _____

2. liturgy _____

3. rites _____

Choose one of the questions below and write a brief paragraph to answer your choice.

4. What is the role of the liturgy in the prayer life of the Church?

_____

_____

5. Describe how popular devotions and sacred images enrich the prayer life of Catholics.

_____

_____

Reflect

Using what you have learned in this chapter, reflect on and describe in your own words the meaning of this statement:

Prayer is a surge of the heart toward God.   SAINT THÉRÈSE OF THE CHILD JESUS

_____

_____

Share

Share with a friend how you make prayer a daily habit. Encourage one another to pray daily.

WITH MY FAMILY

Discuss with your family how prayer strengthens your relationships with one another and with God.

To Help You REMEMBER

1. Praying with the Church is an essential part of our lives.

2. Jesus is our greatest teacher in how to pray.

3. Popular devotions and sacred images enrich the lives of Catholics.

Prayer
before a
CRUCIFIX

Leader: Let us listen to Jesus' prayer to his Father, which he prayed aloud from the Cross.

Reader 1: *Proclaim Luke 23:32–34.*

Reader 2: *Proclaim Luke 23:44–49.*

Leader: The crucifix is a sacred image that reminds us of the infinite love of Christ. Spend a few minutes in silent prayer before the crucifix. Conclude by quietly praying this prayer.

All: Good and gentle Jesus,
I see and ponder your five wounds.
My eyes behold what King David
prophesied about you:
"They have pierced my hands and feet;
they have counted all my bones."
Engrave on me the image of yourself.
Fulfill the yearnings of my heart:
give me faith, hope, and love,
true sorrow for my sins,
and true conversion of life. Amen.

NAME _____

Ⓐ Choose the Best Word

Answer each question by circling the best answer.

1. Which Pope called the bishops together for the Second Vatican Council?

    A. Pope Benedict XVI

    B. Pope John Paul II

    C. Pope John XXIII

    D. Pope Francis

2. What do we call the people of the Church who are not ordained or consecrated religious?

    A. laypeople

    B. bishops

    C. priests

    D. deacons

3. What are the Four Marks of the Church?

    A. one, holy, faithful, catholic

    B. one, holy, moral, catholic

    C. one, holy, catholic, apostolic

    D. one, catholic, faithful, apostolic

4. What is the term the Church uses to name the connection of all Popes and bishops back to Saint Peter and the other Apostles?

    A. apostolic succession

    B. faith connection

    C. deposit of faith

    D. none of the above

5. What is the vocation of all Christians?

    A. to share in the work of the Church

    B. to share in the Paschal Mystery

    C. to be happy with God forever

    D. all of the above

B Show What You Know

Match the item in Column A with those in Column B.

Column A

_____ **1.** meditation

_____ **2.** infallibility

_____ **3.** contemplation

_____ **4.** devotions

_____ **5.** Magisterium

_____ **6.** vocal prayer

_____ **7.** doxologies

_____ **8.** temple of the Holy Spirit

_____ **9.** liturgy

_____ **10.** ecumenism

Column B

A. the indwelling of the Holy Spirit in the Church

B. the teaching authority of the Church

C. prayer and work for restoring unity of the Church

D. acts of individual or communal prayer that rise out of the liturgy

E. the charism that guarantees that the official teaching of the Church on matters of faith and morals is without error

F. the work and worship of the whole people of God

G. prayer spoken out loud or in the quiet of one's heart

H. using one's mind, heart, imagination, and emotions to express the desire to follow Christ

I. praise words that conclude many liturgical prayers

J. taking time to be alone with God

C Connect with Scripture

Reread the Scripture passage on the first Unit Opener page. What connection do you see between this passage and what you learned in this unit?

_____

_____

_____

D Be a Disciple

1. *Review The Church Follows Jesus in each of the chapters. Which person or ministry has inspired you to be a better disciple of Jesus? Explain your response.*

_____

_____

_____

2. *Work with a group. Review the six Disciple Power habits you have learned about in this unit. After jotting down your own ideas, share with the group practical ways that you will live these day by day.*

_____

_____

_____

In Memory of Me

When the hour came, he took his place at table with the apostles. He said to them, "I have eagerly desired to eat this Passover with you before I suffer, for, I tell you, I shall not eat it [again] until there is fulfillment in the kingdom of God." Then he took a cup, gave thanks, and said, "Take this and share it among yourselves; for I tell you [that] from this time on I shall not drink of the fruit of the vine until the kingdom of God comes." Then he took the bread, said the blessing, broke it, and gave it to them, saying, "This is my body, which will be given for you; do this in memory of me." And likewise the cup after they had eaten, saying, "This cup is the new covenant in my blood, which will be shed for you." LUKE 22:14–20

What I Already Know

Complete the following sentences.

The Seven Sacraments are . . .

_____

_____

_____

The Eucharist is . . .

_____

_____

_____

The Sacraments at the Service of Communion are . . .

_____

_____

_____

Faith Vocabulary

With a partner, take turns choosing words and defining them for each other. If there are words that neither of you can define, put a check mark next to them.

_____ **Order of the Mass**

_____ **sacramentals**

_____ **liturgical year**

_____ **source and summit**

_____ **mercy**

_____ **symbols of the Sacraments**

_____ **contrition**

_____ **Anointing of the Sick**

What I Want to Know

Write a question you have under each heading.

Sacred Scripture
What would you like to know about the Beatitudes?

_____

_____

_____

The Church
What would you like to know about the Rites of the Sacraments?

_____

_____

_____

Another Question I Have

_____

_____

_____

LOOKING AHEAD
In this chapter the Holy Spirit invites you to ▶

EXPLORE the lives of two devoted saints.
DISCOVER how the Sacraments developed over time.
DECIDE on how your life can be a sign of God's presence.

CHAPTER **7**

HISTORY of the SACRAMENTS

▶ In what ways has your understanding of the Church developed over time?

Throughout the Church's history, she has come to an ever-greater understanding of God and his ways, especially through the Sacraments. We belong to the pilgrim Church, making us a "pilgrim people." We are on a journey of faithful discovery.

[W]herever you lodge I will lodge, your people shall be my people, and your God my God. RUTH 1:16

▶ What does it mean to you to be a pilgrim people?

TIMELINE

	1221–1274 Life of St. Bonaventure	1515–1582 Life of St. Teresa of Jesus		1567–1622 Life of St. Francis de Sales
1000	1200	1300	1500	1600
1123–1215 Lateran Councils I-IV			1545–1648 Catholic (Counter) Reformation	

Devoted Life

Throughout the Church's history, the Holy Spirit has sent brilliant and dedicated women and men who through their own holy lives offer the faithful ways to enter more deeply into the mystery of God's plan of Salvation. Their insights can help us better understand the mysteries of our faith, such as the Sacraments.

Francis de Sales

Francis de Sales (1567–1622) felt a call to the priesthood from his earliest years. His love for God and his commitment to humble service was so evident that Francis was named bishop of Geneva, Switzerland.

As bishop, Francis saw many of the Catholics in Geneva convert to Calvinism. Francis believed that his most important duty as a bishop was to provide spiritual direction to the people entrusted to his care. Beginning as a series of letters and later published as a book in 1608, his *An Introduction to the Devout Life* gives clear instruction on how to enter more deeply into the mysteries of the Catholic faith. His insights continue to inspire and instruct the faithful today. In this excerpt, Francis offers a beautiful vision of Heaven:

"Jesus Christ looks at you lovingly, from the heights of Heaven, and gently invites you: 'Come, dear one, to everlasting rest in the arms of my goodness. In the abundance of my love, I have prepared for you never-ending delights.' See, with the eyes of your spirit, our Lady inviting you with a mother's love: 'Courage my child. Do not despise my Son's desires, nor my great concern for you, since with him I long for your eternal salvation.' Look at the Saints who earnestly request you, and a million faithful who gently invite you, only desiring to see one day your heart united to theirs to praise God forever."

▶ How have you devoted yourself to Jesus?

Teresa of Jesus

Teresa of Jesus (Teresa of Ávila, 1515–1582) was born in Spain and became a Carmelite nun in 1537. Teresa wanted to follow God perfectly; but as she looked around her monastery, she wondered, "How can I follow God perfectly here?" Monasteries were supposed to be quiet places that encouraged holiness, but her monastery was full of noise. The nuns fixed their hair in the latest styles and wore expensive jewelry. They had frequent visitors and parties.

Teresa decided changes were needed. She believed the nuns should return to a simple life of poverty and humility. Reforming the monastery was not easy because many nuns fiercely opposed Teresa's efforts. Teresa met so much hostility that she complained about her troubles to the Lord. According to one story, in the midst of her frustrations, Teresa is supposed to have said to God once in prayer; "Do you know why you do not have more followers? Look at the way you treat your friends!"

Through prayer and persistence, Teresa overcame the obstacles she faced and established a Carmelite monastery that put her reforms into practice. The monastery was small and poor, but disciplined. Within this prayerful atmosphere, she wrote many reflections on the spiritual life intended to help the faithful gain a greater understanding of the nature of prayer. In one of her most well-known works, *The Interior Castle*, she wrote:

"In a state of grace the soul is like a well of limpid water, from which flow only streams of clearest crystal. Its works are pleasing both to God and man, rising from the River of Life, beside which it is rooted like a tree. Otherwise it would produce neither leaves nor fruit, for the waters of grace nourish it, keep it from withering from drought, and cause it to bring forth good fruit."

Disciple POWER

HUMILITY
The humble person has an honest understanding of his or her gifts and weaknesses and is comfortable with who he or she is. Humble people do not hesitate to place their gifts at the service of the Church and of the world.

FAITH JOURNAL

Describe a time when you were frustrated with God. How did you handle it?

_____

_____

_____

_____

_____

_____

_____

_____

► FAITH FOCUS

How have the Sacraments developed over the years?

► FAITH VOCABULARY

apostates

Christendom

mendicant

Christian Initiation

The Seven Sacraments have been a part of the life of the Church since the beginning. Through the centuries, however, the ways in which they are administered have changed. Sometimes these changes happened to better meet the needs of the faithful. Other times, changes occurred as our understanding of how God works through the Sacraments deepened.

In the early Church Baptism, Confirmation, and the Eucharist were usually administered together. This was done because most people who became Christians were already adults. After going through a period of preparation (catechesis), those wanting to become part of the Church were baptized and confirmed in the presence of the entire community during the Easter Vigil Mass. Then for the first time they would receive the Body and Blood of Jesus in the Eucharist.

Sacramental Life

Celebration of the Liturgy of Saint James, oldest Eucharistic liturgy in continuous use

Catholics BELIEVE

The *First Apology* of Saint Justin reveals that the order of the Mass celebrated in the second century remains similar to today's Mass. Saint Justin wrote that on Sunday Christians gather in one place, the Scriptures are read, a homily is preached, donations for the poor are collected, bread and wine and water are brought forth, the celebrant prays and gives thanks, the people respond "Amen," and Holy Communion is distributed.

By 395 most of the citizens and subjects of the Roman Empire were Christians. This fundamental change, along with a growing concern for children who might die without Baptism, eventually resulted in the Baptism of infants becoming the norm in the Roman Catholic Church.

▶ Why would a person want to receive the Sacrament of Confirmation?

Celebrating the Eucharist

The rites used in the celebration of Mass took shape in the days of the early Church rather quickly. Much of the way the Church celebrates the Eucharistic liturgy has its roots in Jewish rituals. The mission to the Gentiles, however, introduced a number of changes in the way early Christians worshipped. Gradually the celebration of the Eucharist became more and more distinct from Jewish rituals and worship.

Saint Justin Martyr's (d. 165) *First Apology* (c. 148–155) describes the way the Mass was celebrated in the early Church. The order, or structure, of the Mass has essentially remained the same throughout the centuries. Both Jews and Christians honor the living Word of God as revealed in Sacred Scripture. Of course as Christians, we believe God's Word is found in both the Old Testament and the New Testament. And the Mass culminates in the Eucharist, the memorial of Christ's Paschal Mystery, the work of our Salvation.

Faith CONNECTION

Describe to a friend or partner one of your most memorable experiences of celebrating the Mass.

Ruins of Cistercian Jerpoint Abbey, Jerpoint, County Kilkenny, Leinster, Republic of Ireland

Celebrating Reconciliation

By the 4th century most Christian persecutions in the Roman Empire had ended. Many baptized Christians who had publically denied their faith during the persecutions, known as **apostates**, wanted to return to full communion with the Church. After much debate and turmoil, the practice of a one-time public penance was used for these apostates to express their sorrow to the community and be readmitted into the Church.

Recognizing that at the core of the Gospel message is repentance and forgiveness, the Church gradually expanded upon this public penance into the form we are familiar with today in the Rite of Penance.

Saint Columba

Saint Columba (521–597) spent many years traveling about Ireland and Scotland, preaching the Gospel and establishing monasteries. One of the most enduring legacies of Columba is his influence on the development of the Sacrament of Penance and Reconciliation. He helped establish the practice of private confession and the granting of absolution by a priest. Eventually this practice of penance spread throughout the world where the Church was established. This is the form that the Rite of Penance follows today.

▶ Would you have let the apostates back into the Church? Why or why not?

Holy Orders

By the twelfth century the Church, especially through the papacy, became the dominant influence in Western Civilization. The Lateran Councils in Rome (1123, 1139, 1179, and 1215) are some recorded signs of the resurgence of the papacy during this period. By the turn of the first millennium, the Gospel had been preached virtually throughout all of Western Europe. The term **Christendom** refers to this vast growth of Christianity both in territory populated by Christians, and in political and spiritual power. The result was that Church authority in the West often surpassed that of the emperors.

Beginning with Pope Saint Leo IX (1002–1054), the next several centuries were filled with events and people calling the Church to renewal. It was during these centuries that celibacy became a requirement for those baptized men receiving the Sacrament of Holy Orders.

Celibacy, the promise that a priest makes to commit his life only to the Church and never to marry, was always encouraged among the clergy as a means to give witness to the Kingdom of God.

This discipline of celibacy allows the minister to focus his energies on the needs of the people. It became a law of the Church during this period in part to ensure that those entering into Holy Orders fully understood and accepted the ministry of service.

DID YOU KNOW?

During Jesus' time, one custom was that a visitor was to wash his feet upon entering a house because the roads were dusty. Usually there would be a bowl with water by the door for this purpose. If the family was wealthy, a servant might be assigned the chore. For a person of higher social standing (such as a teacher) to perform this menial task would be a most unusual gesture.

Faith CONNECTION

Which qualities do you think a man needs to be a priest?

Council of Trent, fresco by brothers Taddeo and Federico Zuccari, in Hall of Farnesina Magnificience of Palazzo Farnese, Caprarola, Italy, 1560–1566

Catholic Reformation

In the twelfth and thirteenth centuries, social stability was returning to Europe, commerce and urban centers were reviving, and learning was once again possible outside the monasteries. Schools developed where theologians, called Scholastics, used human reason to explain the teachings of the Church. Among the most famous of the Scholastics were Thomas Aquinas (c.1225–1274), a Dominican, and Bonaventure (1221–1274), a Franciscan.

There were many holy women and men who helped reform the Church during the late Middle Ages and early Renaissance (1200–1500). A follower of Saint Francis and Saint Dominic became known as a **mendicant**. The word *mendicant* comes from a Latin word meaning "to beg." These Franciscans and Dominicans traveled about preaching the Gospel. As they traveled they begged for food and lodging.

By the 16th century the Church experienced great reform. At the Council of Trent (1545-1563), the Catholic Church developed various ways and means to renew the spiritual health of the pilgrim Church and to clarify and reassert her doctrinal teachings.

The Council of Trent initiated a number of reforms and clarifications of Church teaching in the area of Sacred Scripture, the creation of the first catechism (book used to teach the faithful about the Church) and the formation of priests. The Council for the first time in Church history set the number of the Sacraments at seven, and defined the seven in the way we still do today: Baptism, Confirmation, the Eucharist, Penance and Reconciliation, Anointing of the Sick, Matrimony and Holy Orders.

Faith CONNECTION

Explain to a partner the importance of each Sacrament you have received.

Herald and SERVANT

As a member of the Church, you are called to join with all the baptized and be a herald and a servant of the Gospel. A Christian herald proclaims and invites others to accept the Good News of God's love revealed in Jesus Christ. A Christian servant serves and helps others as Christ did.

There are many ways that you can fulfill your responsibility to be a herald of the Gospel. Here are a few suggestions:

- Show by your words and actions that you are a disciple of Jesus Christ.

- Share with others the teachings of the Catholic Church and demonstrate that the Catholic faith makes a difference.

- Share your faith with your classmates through social media.

- Support a missionary or a missionary community by writing letters, collecting money, or donating food and clothing.

- Volunteer to be an altar server or lector at Mass. Be active in your parish.

IN SERVICE
TO OTHERS

Here are some ways that you can fulfill your baptismal call to serve the Church and others.

- Volunteer to be part of a school or parish project that reaches out to people in need; for example, people needing food, clothing, or housing.

- Help out at home without being asked; volunteer for chores that no one else wants to do.

- Tutor or coach younger children; take part in a babysitting group in your parish.

- Help a classmate who has been sick to catch up with schoolwork.

▶ Work in a small group to brainstorm ways to be heralds and servants of the Gospel. Choose one way to decide how your group will work together to put this idea into action.

MY FAITH CHOICE

This week to help me become a better herald and servant of the Gospel, I will:

_____

_____ .

 PRAY Lord, you are the source of strength. Help me to serve the Church in her mission, and to be a herald of your Word. Amen.

Recall

Define each of these faith terms:

1. apostate _____

2. Christendom _____

3. mendicant _____

Choose one of the questions below and write a brief paragraph to answer your choice.

4. Discuss how the Church responded to the Protestant Reformation.

_____

_____

5. Describe how a Saint has contributed to the Church's work of renewal and reform.

_____

_____

To Help You
REMEMBER

1. Throughout the centuries, the Church's understanding of the Sacraments has deepened.

2. Some of the ways in which we celebrate the Sacraments have changed according to the needs of the faithful.

3. The Sacraments of Christian Initiation celebrate full communion into the Church.

Reflect

Using what you have learned in this chapter, reflect on and describe in your own words the meaning of this statement:

By the power of the risen Lord [the Church] is given strength that it might, in patience and in love, overcome its sorrows and its challenges, both within itself and from without, and that it might reveal to the world, faithfully though darkly, the mystery of its Lord until, in the end, it will be manifested in full light.

LUMEN GENTIUM [DOGMATIC CONSTITUTION ON THE CHURCH], 8

Share

With a partner learn more about the Council of Trent. List here three important teachings from this council.

_____

_____

_____

WITH MY FAMILY

Discuss with your family how you all live as a "pilgrim people"?

Praise to GOD

Leader: We are a sacramental people because we rejoice in the presence of God in all of creation. Together, let us pray with the psalmist:

Group 1: When I behold your heavens, the work of your fingers, the moon and the stars which you set in place.

Group 2: What are humans that you should be mindful of them, mere mortals that you should care for them?

Group 1: You have made them little less than a god, crowned them with glory and honor.

Group 2: You have given them rule over the works of your hands, putting all things at their feet: All sheep and oxen, even the beasts of the field,

Group 1: The birds of the air, the fish of the sea, and whatever swims the paths of the seas.

All: Lord how awesome is your name over all the Earth!

BASED ON PSALM 8:4–10

LOOKING AHEAD
In this chapter the Holy
Spirit invites you to ▶

EXPLORE the lives of two influential Popes.
DISCOVER how the liturgy brings us closer to God.
DECIDE how to be more mindful of God's presence today.

CHAPTER **8**

Give Thanks
to the Lord

▶ **What do you spend most of your time focused on?**

The things to which we give the most attention have a major influence on how we live our lives. God is to be the focus, or center, of our lives. We celebrate and remind ourselves of this essential truth when we celebrate the Mass.

Your word is a lamp for my feet,
a light for my path. PSALM 119:105

▶ **How does the Mass help light your path to see God?**

TIMELINE

1969 Paul VI revises the Roman Missal.	**2007** Tridentine Mass becomes extraordinary form.	**2011** Third English translation of the Roman Missal

1800	1900	2000	2100

1976 First spiral compact fluorescent light bulb

2007 World's first OLED TV

Influential Popes

Throughout the history of the Church, the Holy Spirit has raised up a number of great leaders and reformers in the Church. Many have distinguished themselves as noble leaders of the Church who had great love for the liturgical and sacramental life of the Church.

Gregory the Great

As Rome's power declined and barbarians attacked the Roman Empire, the Church stepped in and established leadership. One of the Church's most effective leaders was Gregory the Great who became Pope in 590. He negotiated an agreement for peace with the barbarian invaders. Pope Gregory knew that to maintain a peaceful society, the barbarians would have to become Christians.

Many Christian practices, which were rich in symbolism and tradition, naturally appealed to the barbarians. So the liturgy and the Sacraments of the Church were appealing to the barbarian invaders who had settled within the Roman Empire. At a time when illiteracy was widespread, Pope Gregory encouraged a new type of music based on the chanting of hymns and prayers by a choir. This musical prayer came to be known as "Gregorian chant" and has greatly enhanced the beauty of the Mass. Pope Gregory's prudent leadership helped revitalize the spiritual life of the Church.

▶ If you were asked to suggest one reform on how to celebrate the Mass, what would it be?

Benedict XVI

Pope Benedict XVI was born Joseph Ratzinger on Holy Saturday in 1927, in Bavaria, Germany. When World War II ended, Joseph, along with his brother Georg, finished their priestly formation. They were both ordained to the priesthood in 1951.

In 1977, Father Joseph Ratzinger was named Archbishop of Munich and Friesing. He chose as his motto the phrase "Collaborator of the Truth." Not long after being named archbishop, he was elevated by Pope Paul VI to the rank of cardinal.

In response to Cardinal Ratzinger's obvious love for the liturgy and the Sacraments along with his unfailing commitment to teach people the truth about God and the Church, Pope John Paul II named him the Prefect of the Congregation for the Doctrine of the Faith. In this role, Cardinal Ratzinger encouraged more reverent and prayerful liturgical celebrations by ensuring that related Church teachings were correctly explained to the faithful.

In 2005, Cardinal Ratzinger was elected Pope, and took the name Benedict XVI. Under his pontificate, Catholics throughout the United States and Canada received a new English translation of the *Roman Missal*. The prayers of the Mass were given an updated translation to help better connect the faithful to the beauty and meaning of the original Latin, which serves as the official language of the Church. In shepherding this change, Pope Benedict XVI prudently communicated the central importance of celebrating the Eucharist.

FAITH JOURNAL

Describe your favorite aspect of the Mass.

_____

_____

_____

_____

_____

_____

_____

_____

_____

To the Father

Jesus focused his earthly life on doing the will of the Father. Joined to Christ at Baptism, we too are called to focus our attention on God. When we gather together as the new People of God during the Mass, we join with Christ, the Head of the Church. Through the power of the Holy Spirit we give thanks and praise to God the Father as the source of all the blessings of creation and Salvation.

WORSHIPPING GOD

By spending time with the Father and focusing on his love, we share more fully in the life of God, and we welcome him into our lives. We see and appreciate that from the beginning of time God has always done and will continue to do what is good for us.

With the Son

Through the work of the liturgy, Christ's work of Salvation is made present and carried out among us. Christ is always present and leads his Church in the celebration of the liturgy.

- Christ is present in the priest, who acts in the Person of Christ.

- Christ is present in the assembly.

- Christ is present in the living Word of God, the Scriptures.

- Christ is present, most importantly, in the Eucharist under the appearances of bread and wine.

It is always "through him, with him, and in him, / O God, almighty Father, / in the unity of the Holy Spirit . . ." (Doxology, Eucharistic Prayer) that we give praise and thanks to the Father.

▶ **When and where do you feel closest to God? Why?**

Through the Holy Spirit

The mission, or work, attributed to the Holy Spirit is to make us sharers in God's life. In the liturgy the Holy Spirit does this in four ways:

- The Holy Spirit prepares us to meet Christ and join with him. The Holy Spirit prepares our hearts to accept God's gift of himself and to share in God's saving plan of Salvation.

- The Holy Spirit opens our minds and hearts to accept God's Word.

- The Holy Spirit makes the saving work of Christ present and real to us by his transforming power.

- The Holy Spirit, especially through the Eucharist, brings us into communion with Christ and one another.

The ultimate work of the Holy Spirit is to draw us more deeply into the mystery and reality of the Holy Trinity, and into loving relationship with one another.

Faith CONNECTION

Draw how you visualize the Holy Trinity.

DID YOU KNOW?

The earliest written mention of the Trinitarian formula is found in the Gospel of Matthew. As part of Jesus' final instructions to his Apostles, a passage referred to as the "Great Commissioning," Jesus exhorts: "(baptize) in the name of the Father, and of the Son, and of the holy Spirit" (Mt 28:19). Many biblical scholars think that this passage might be preserved from an early baptismal rite of the Church.

Share in Mystery

The Paschal Mystery is the saving events of the Passion, Death, Resurrection, and glorious Ascension of Jesus Christ. The Sacraments make us sharers in the Paschal Mystery. Through this mystery we have been drawn into and made sharers in the mystery of the divine life of the Holy Trinity.

The celebration of Christ's Paschal Mystery in the liturgy and Sacraments is unique. A sacrament is an effective sign instituted by Christ and entrusted to the Church, by which **grace**, or the divine life of God, is shared with us. Through our participation in the celebration of the Sacraments, our lives are changed, or transformed, and we become sharers in the life of God. The Church celebrates Seven Sacraments, which are classified into three groups:

1. Sacraments of Christian Initiation: Baptism, Confirmation, and Eucharist

2. Sacraments of Healing: Penance and Reconciliation, and Anointing of the Sick

3. Sacraments at the Service of Communion: Holy Orders and Matrimony

The three Sacraments of Baptism, Confirmation, and Holy Orders each imprint on the person who receives these Sacraments an indelible, or permanent, character that remains forever. This is the reason a person can receive these Sacraments only one time.

▶ How do you understand Baptism uniting us to Christ and the Church?

Common Elements

There are certain common characteristics, or elements, that all the Sacraments share. These characteristics help us understand why the Sacraments are necessary for the Salvation of believers.

- Christ is the principal celebrant of every Sacrament. All Sacraments are instituted, or given to us, by Christ.

- A Sacrament is an effective sign of grace. This means that each Sacrament actually accomplishes what it signifies. This happens even if the human minister of the Sacrament is unworthy.

- The celebration of a Sacrament is both the work of Christ and the work of the Church. The ordained minister of the Church— bishop, priest, or deacon—leads the celebration of a Sacrament. Ordained to serve the Church, he acts in the name and Person of Christ.

- The Sacraments are sensible signs of the Holy Spirit's work.

Rites of the Sacraments

Each of the Sacraments has a rite approved by the Church for its celebration. A rite is the way something is regularly done. The words and actions the Church uses to celebrate a Sacrament is called the rite of that Sacrament.

The rite used for the celebration of each Sacrament has many parts. Some of these parts are divinely given and are unchangeable. For example, during the Eucharistic Prayer, the priest says the words, "TAKE THIS, ALL OF YOU, AND EAT OF IT, / FOR THIS IS MY BODY, / WHICH WILL BE GIVEN UP FOR YOU" (Eucharistic Prayer *Roman Missal*).

The rite of a Sacrament also has parts that the Church can adapt and change. For example, before Vatican Council II (1962–1965), Latin, the official language of the Church, was the most widely used language in the celebration of the liturgy by the Roman Catholic Church. Today Mass is celebrated in each country around the world using the vernacular, or the common language used by the people.

DID YOU KNOW?

There are three days in the Fall that when viewed together celebrate the wonderful mystery known as the Communion of Saints On October 31, All Hallows Eve (Halloween), it is traditional to celebrate a Vigil Mass in preparation for All Saints on November 1st. November 2 is All Souls' Day, on which we are especially mindful of those souls who need our prayers.

Faith CONNECTION

Create a chart listing the Parts of the Mass. Then under each, identify how the Mass changes from week to week.

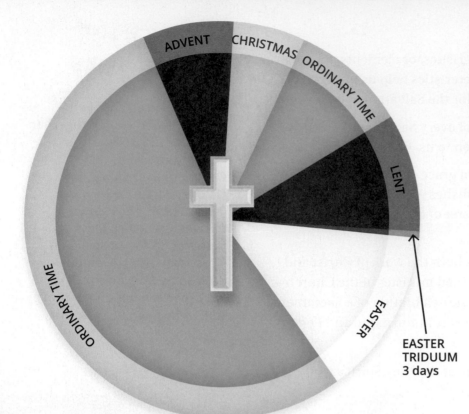

Advent and Christmas. During the liturgical seasons of Advent and Christmas, we prepare for and celebrate the Incarnation, the Nativity, and the announcement of Jesus as the Savior of the world.

Lent, Easter Triduum, and Easter. During Lent the elect (catechumens) prepare for their initiation into the Church. All the faithful join with them and renew their own baptismal promises. The whole Church prepares for the celebration of Christ's Passion, Death, and Resurrection. Holy Thursday, Good Friday, and the celebration of Easter Vigil/Easter Sunday are the most important days of the liturgical year. We call these days—which begin with the celebration of the evening Mass of the Lord's Supper and conclude with Vespers on Easter Sunday—the Easter Triduum, or simply the Triduum, a term which means three days.

Ordinary Time. The longest part of the liturgical year is called Ordinary Time. The word ordinary comes from a Latin word meaning "number." On these numbered weeks of the year—for example, the Thirteenth Sunday in Ordinary Time—we listen to the events of the public ministry of Jesus and respond to his invitation to live as his disciples.

Solemnities, Feasts, and Memorials. The Church also celebrates an annual cycle of feasts. These include the holy days of obligation and other days, such as the Solemnity of Our Lord Jesus Christ, King of the Universe, and days remembering Mary, the Apostles, and the other Saints.

Changing Elements

As we gather to celebrate the Eucharist each Sunday, we notice that throughout the year the color of the priest's and deacon's vestments changes. We may see green, white, purple (or violet), or red. Hymns and readings change too. All these changing elements help us recognize the feast or season of the **liturgical year** we are celebrating. Paying attention to the cycle of seasons and feasts of the liturgical year and to their meanings will greatly enhance our participation.

Sunday. Sunday is the weekly celebration of the Resurrection. This is the Lord's Day. From the days of the early Church, Sunday has been ranked as the first holy day of all.

BEING CLOSE to GOD

One of the wonderful truths of our faith is that God is always present with us. He is not only In Heaven, but is right here within each person. The Catholic Church—through the liturgy, the Sacraments, and sacramentals—makes us aware of and encourages us to respond to the constant, loving presence of God in our daily lives.

There are times when you may be very aware of the closeness of God. Then there are times when you just get so wrapped up in what's going on that you totally forget that God is right here—right now.

▶ How can you develop the daily habit of recognizing God, thanking him, and praising him for his loving presence?

AWARENESS OF GOD'S PRESENCE

Here are a few steps to develop an awareness of God's presence.

- Become more conscious of your surroundings. Look for the beauty in God's creation. Say a conscious, deliberate thank-you to God for the wonders of creation.

- Take time to appreciate the gifts God has given you. Think of ways to show God your appreciation for these gifts.

- Remember in times of trouble that God is with you. Ask God to give you the courage, strength, and comfort you need.

- As you encounter people try to remind yourself that every person is a child of God. Thank God for the people in your life and ask God to bless them.

MY FAITH CHOICE

This week I will make a deliberate choice to be aware of God's presence in my life. I will:

_____

_____ .

 PRAY Lord, help me to cherish all that you have given. Amen.

Recall

Define each of these faith terms:

1. grace _____

2. liturgical year _____

3. Sacrament _____

Choose one of the questions below and write a brief paragraph to answer your choice.

4. Explain the work of the Holy Trinity in the Mass.

_____

_____

5. Describe three ways Christ is present in the Mass.

_____

_____

_____

Reflect

Using what you have learned in this chapter, reflect on and describe in your own words the meaning of this statement:

Sacraments are "powers that come forth" from the Body of Christ, which is ever-living and life-giving. They are "the masterwork of God" in the new and everlasting covenant.

CATECHISM OF THE CATHOLIC CHURCH 1116

_____

_____

Share

Discuss with a partner how you participate in the sacramental life of the Church.

WITH MY FAMILY

Discuss with your family: How does participating in the Mass help us keep God at the center of our family?

To Help You REMEMBER

1. The Mass is our worship to God the Father, with the Son, through the Holy Spirit.

2. The Seven Sacraments are the means by which Christ shares grace with us.

3. The liturgical year is the cycle of seasons and feasts the Church celebrates each year.

Acclaim the LORD

Group 1: You are God: we praise you; You are the Lord: we acclaim you; You are the eternal Father: all creation worships you.

Group 2: To all you angels, all the powers of heaven, Cherubim and Seraphim, sing in endless praise:

All: **Holy, Holy, Holy Lord, God of hosts. Heaven and earth are full of your glory.**

Group 1: Day by day we bless you. We praise your name for ever.

Group 2: Keep us today from all sin. Have mercy on us; Lord, have mercy.

All: **Lord, show us your love and mercy; for we put our trust in you. In you, Lord, is our hope; and we shall never hope in vain. Amen.**

LOOKING AHEAD
In this chapter the Holy Spirit invites you to ▶

EXPLORE the courageous lives of two Saints.
DISCOVER more about Baptism and Confirmation.
DECIDE on how to live out your baptismal promises.

CHAPTER **9**

Baptism and Confirmation

▶ Have you been initiated into any groups? What was that initiation like?

The word *initiation* comes from the Latin word meaning "beginning." Sometimes we talk about being initiated into a group. We begin to be members of that group. In the Catholic Church, initiation refers to the time when we begin new life in Jesus Christ and the Church.

To each individual the manifestation of the Spirit is given for some benefit.

1 CORINTHIANS 12:7

▶ Describe what you know about the celebration of your own Baptism.

TIMELINE						
	1562–1597 Life of St. Paul Miki		1610–1611 Ruben's *The Elevation of the Cross*	1656–1680 Life of St. Kateri Tekakwitha		
1550		1600	1650	1700		1800
	1555 Peace of Augsburg					1794 Treaty of Canandaigua

Cultures of Faith

Women and men from all over the world have lived out their baptismal promises and given witness to their relationship with Jesus. Two such models of faith are Kateri Tekakwitha and Paul Miki.

Paul Miki

In 1562, Paul Miki was born in Japan. At the age of eighteen, he answered the call to religious life by joining the Society of Jesus, or the Jesuits. He became well known for his preaching style, and continued to preach even when Japanese leaders began to strongly oppose Christianity.

Eventually, Paul was arrested for spreading Christ's message. With twenty-five other Catholic men, Paul marched 600 miles to Nagasaki to spread the Gospel. On February 5, 1597, the Japanese leaders crucified Paul, along with two other Jesuits, six Franciscans, and seventeen laypeople.

As he was dying, Paul remained committed to his faith. He gave this final speech from his cross: "The only reason for my being killed is that I have taught the doctrine of Christ. I thank God it is for this reason that I die. I believe that I am telling the truth before I die. I know you believed me and I want to say to you all once again: Ask Christ to help you become happy." In 1862, Pope Pius IX canonized Paul Miki and those faithful who died with him. Saint Paul Miki's feast day is February 6.

▶ What is the hardest thing that you have had to do for your faith?

Kateri Tekakwitha

Kateri Tekakwitha was born in 1656 in what is now New York state. She was a member of the Iroquois Nation. In Mohawk Tekakwitha means "she puts things in order."

When Tekakwitha was twelve years old, Jesuit missionaries came to her village. They asked the permission of the tribe's chief to tell the people about God. They promised to visit in peace. Tekakwitha listened to their stories and began to believe. On Easter of 1676, she responded to the call of God, and was baptized. She took the name Kateri, which is Mohawk for "Catherine."

Some of the people in her village felt that Kateri had betrayed them by being baptized. They called her a "Christian dog" and tried to scare her. She remained patient and kind, but eventually saw that she had to leave her family and village.

She decided to go to another village, called the "prayer fort," where everyone was Christian.

In the "prayer fort," Kateri was happy. She was skilled at bead work and made beautiful things to put in the chapel. She did not marry because she wanted to live for God alone. The whole village was Kateri's family. She was a good storyteller who held everyone's attention when she told the stories of Jesus. When she prayed, her face would light up as if she were actually seeing God. She became known as the Lily of the Mohawks.

Kateri's health failed, and she died at age twenty-four. After she died, her face became radiant. The Native Americans felt this showed how much God loved Kateri. Jesuit missionaries who knew Kateri well left a written record of her life and spirituality. The Church celebrates Saint Kateri Tekakwitha's life on April 17 in Canada and July 14 in the United States. She is the first native North American Saint.

FAITH JOURNAL

Where is your "prayer fort" or place that you prefer to pray?

▶ **FAITH FOCUS**

How do Baptism and Confirmation transform us?

▶ **FAITH VOCABULARY**

Baptism

Confirmation

Sacraments of Christian Initiation

Christian Initiation

Christian initiation is our entrance into the Church. Through the three **Sacraments of Christian Initiation**, we are joined to Christ. In the celebration of Baptism, Confirmation, and the Eucharist, we are made sharers in God's life. Because we are joined to Christ, we belong to his Body, the Church (see 1 Corinthians 12:27, Colossians 1:18).

An initiation is a new beginning. Baptism, Confirmation, and Eucharist lay the foundation for the Christian life and mark a new beginning. They join us to Christ. By making us members of his Body, they also join us to the Church.

Baptism is the beginning of our new life in Christ. Confirmation is its strengthening. And the Eucharist nourishes us with Christ's Body and Blood for our transformation in Christ. In this chapter we will study Baptism and Confirmation.

Baptism is the chief Sacrament of forgiveness. This Sacrament marks a new beginning by canceling, or wiping out, all sin in our lives, whether Original Sin or personal sins (see Acts 2:38).

▶ **How has your family nurtured your faith in the Catholic Church?**

Belonging to **Christ**

New Birth

Baptism is our birth into new life in Christ (see 1 Peter 1:23). In Baptism we receive the gift of the Holy Spirit, who enables us to believe in Christ and live the Gospel. Through the Holy Spirit, we become adopted sons and daughters of God the Father in the Son, Jesus. In other words, through Baptism we become adopted children of the Father, members of Christ's Body, and temples of the Holy Spirit (see 1 Corinthians 3:16, 6:19; 2 Corinthians 5:17; Ephesians 4:25).

Door to the Church

Baptism is the door and path to the other Sacraments. We can only share in them when we have been first "born of water and the Holy Spirit" (John 3:5). Only when we are joined to Jesus Christ through Baptism can we meet him and be changed by him in the other Sacraments of the Church.

Celebration of Baptism

Perhaps you are already familiar with the celebration of Baptism. The essential parts of the celebration of this first Sacrament include immersing a person three times into blessed water (or pouring it three times over a person's head), while saying the words given to us by Christ:

> (Name), I baptize you
> in the name of the Father,
> and of the Son,
> and of the Holy Spirit.
>
> *RITE OF BAPTISM 148*

Once a person is baptized he or she cannot receive Baptism again. This is because Baptism seals us with a spiritual character that marks us as forever belonging to Christ. This spiritual character is indelible; that is, it cannot be removed or erased even by sin and is a permanent part of who we are. By being baptized, we belong to Christ forever.

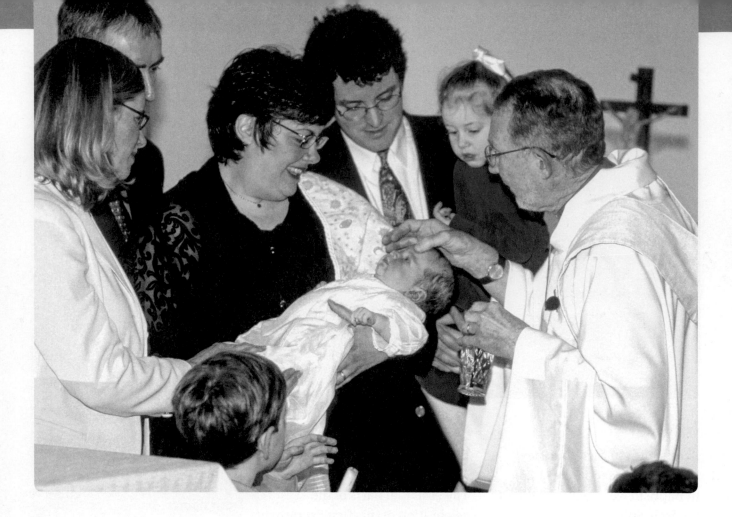

Baptism Q & A

Baptism often generates questions from Catholics and non-Catholics alike. Here are a few frequently asked questions about Baptism and answers to them.

Question: Why are we baptized as infants in the Catholic Church? Why not wait until we can decide for ourselves?

Answer: Infant baptism became the norm in the Church many centuries ago. Scripture includes the account of whole households being baptized, which likely included children. Sharing in the life of Christ is such a remarkable and freely given gift of God that the Church wishes to share it with everyone.

Question: If Baptism is necessary for Salvation, what happens to children who are not baptized?

Answer: The Church entrusts unbaptized children who die to God's mercy. Jesus' tenderness toward children allows us to trust that there is a way of Salvation for God's unbaptized children. The *Catechism of the Catholic Church* reminds us that, "God has bound salvation to the sacrament of Baptism, but he himself is not bound by his sacrament" (CCC 1257).

Question: Are there unbaptized adults who are saved?

Answer: Again, keep in mind that God has bound Salvation to the Sacrament of Baptism, but God is not bound by his sacrament. The Church has always believed that those who die for their faith prior to being baptized are "baptized" by their death for and with Christ. Those preparing for Baptism who die before being baptized are assured of Salvation by virtue of their desire to be baptized. Finally, anyone, who is ignorant of Christ's Gospel and his Church yet seeks God sincerely and strives to fulfill his will, can be saved even if he or she has not been baptized.

Question: Who can perform the Sacrament of Baptism? Or, who is the minister of Baptism?

Answer: The ordinary minister of Baptism is a bishop, priest, or deacon. In cases of necessity, any person may baptize as long as that person performs the rite correctly and with proper intention to baptize someone into the Christian faith.

Question: Does the Catholic Church recognize Christians baptized in other Christian communities as truly baptized?

Answer: Yes, when those Christian communities follow the requirements for a proper celebration of Baptism. Baptism constitutes the foundation of the unity and communion among all Christians. We, the new People of God, are all joined to Christ, the Head of the Church through Baptism.

Question: Is the Sacrament of Baptism ever celebrated together with other Sacraments?

Answer: Yes. The Church celebrates the Rite of Christian Initiation with children of catechetical age (around age seven), older children, teens, and adults. This rite includes steps and periods in the initiation process. These steps and periods culminate in the celebration of Baptism, Confirmation, and Eucharist at the Easter Vigil.

▶ **What further questions do you have about the Sacrament of Baptism?**

DID YOU KNOW?

The practice of bishops conferring the Sacrament of Confirmation is rooted in the earliest days of the Church when local churches were small and the bishop was chosen from the local community. The order of the presbyterate ("priests") evolved as local churches in the cities of the Roman Empire became too big for one bishop to personally "oversee" (the literal meaning of the Greek word for bishop, *episkopos*). Priests initially directly assisted the bishop in supervising the community and eventually became the pastors of local parishes.

The Rite of Confirmation

Confirmation seals the sacramental graces of Baptism. This Sacrament celebrates the special gift of the Holy Spirit. The ordinary minister for Confirmation is a bishop. In some circumstances the local ordinary, or bishop of a diocese, may delegate a priest to confer this Sacrament. Whether Confirmation is administered by a bishop or by a priest, the essential Rite of Confirmation includes laying the minister's hand on the head of the candidate for Confirmation and anointing the candidate's forehead with Sacred Chrism, saying, "Be sealed with the Gift of the Holy Spirit."

Effects of Confirmation

The effects, or sacramental graces, of the Church's celebration of Confirmation in the life of a baptized person are:

- a deepening of our rebirth as adopted children of God the Father

- a unity that is evermore closer to the Lord Jesus

- an increase in the Gifts of the Holy Spirit within us

- the strengthening of the bond of unity we experience with the Church

- and the encouragement to spread and defend the faith by word and deed

The special outpouring of the Holy Spirit that Confirmation represents brings the graces of Baptism to a new depth and fullness in the life of the believer. This is why the sacramental formula speaks of being sealed with "the Gift of the Holy Spirit." Without Confirmation, a person is not fully initiated into the Church. Like Baptism, Confirmation imprints an indelible spiritual mark on the soul, making it a once-in-a-lifetime experience.

All candidates for Confirmation who have attained the age of reason must profess their faith, be in a state of grace, and have the intention of receiving the Sacrament. They must be prepared to assume the role of Christ's disciples and to give witness to their faith in Christ.

Faith CONNECTION

Look up and read one of these Scripture passages: Matthew 16:24–27; Mark 4:1–9; Luke 4:16–22. Summarize what the passage you read teaches about living as a witness for Christ.

Being a Welcoming Person

At Baptism we are all welcomed into the Family of God, the Church. In our own parish communities we welcome those who come to worship each week. How can we practice hospitality and be welcoming to people every day, not just on Sundays and holidays?

Hospitality involves being available, accepting and authentic. It is a way of being that makes the people you greet feel comfortable and at home. Hospitality helps people feel that they belong. Of course, we must always practice caution when we are dealing with total strangers. Let us talk specifically, therefore, about the people we know at school, in our homes, in our neighborhoods, and in our parish communities.

Hospitality is a key characteristic of God's people. Ask yourself the following questions to determine just how hospitable and welcoming a person you are:

- When you pass someone in the hall, do you smile, say hello, or just ignore them?

- When someone new tries to sit with you at lunch, do you warmly receive that person or give him or her a cold shoulder?

- How do you treat the others outside your circle of friends?

WELCOMING OTHERS

While you are not expected to be best friends with every single person whom you encounter, you are expected to be a friendly, cordial, caring, and inviting person. Since God is present in everyone, when you welcome others, you welcome God. Here is a list of ways of being a welcoming person—a person of hospitality:

■ Respect others by accepting them as persons created in the image and likeness of God.

■ Be courteous and considerate. Be generous, not possessive, of your friends' and your time.

■ Build up your self-esteem, but don't put others down or be jealous or push others away.

MY FAITH CHOICE

This week I will focus on being a joyful person by welcoming others whom I encounter. I will:

_____

_____

 PRAY Holy Spirit, strengthen in me the grace to be full of joy when welcoming others. Let your light shine in me. Amen.

Recall

Define each of these faith terms:

1. Baptism _____

2. Confirmation _____

3. Sacraments of Christian Initiation _____

Choose one of the questions below and write a brief paragraph to answer your choice.

4. Describe the essential aspects of the Rite of Baptism.

_____

_____

5. Describe the essential aspects of the Rite of Confirmation.

_____

_____

To Help You
REMEMBER

1. Baptism, Confirmation, and the Eucharist are the Sacraments of Christian Initiation.

2. Through Baptism, we belong to Christ.

3. Through Confirmation, the Holy Spirit strengthens us in a mature faith.

Reflect

Using what you have learned in this chapter, reflect on and describe in your own words the meaning of this statement:

Holy Baptism is the basis of the whole Christian life, the gateway to life in the Spirit, and the door which gives access to the other sacraments.

CATECHISM OF THE CATHOLIC CHURCH 1213

_____

_____

_____

Share

Discuss with a partner how Baptism and Confirmation invite others with joy to belong to the Church.

WITH MY FAMILY

Discuss with your family: How are we living out our baptismal promises?

PROFESSING OUR Faith

Leader : At Baptism we profess the faith of the Church and promise to live that faith. Each Easter Sunday we renew our baptismal promises to serve God faithfully in his holy Catholic Church. Let us profess that faith again today.
Do you believe in God, the Father almighty, creator of Heaven and Earth?

All: I do.

Leader: Do you believe in Jesus Christ, his only Son, our Lord, who was born of the Virgin Mary, was crucified, died, and was buried, rose from the dead, and is now seated at the right hand of the Father?

All: I do.

Leader: Do you believe in the Holy Spirit, the holy Catholic Church, the communion of saints, the forgiveness of sins, the resurrection of the body, and the life everlasting?

All: I do.

BASED ON PROFESSION OF FAITH, RITE OF BAPTISM

Leader: God, our loving Father, send the Holy Spirit to teach us how to live as faithful followers of your Son, Jesus Christ. We ask this in his name.

All: Amen.

LOOKING AHEAD
In this chapter the Holy Spirit invites you to ▶

EXPLORE the difference one group can make in the world.
DISCOVER how we experience Jesus in the Eucharist.
DECIDE how to foster a spirit of thanksgiving.

CHAPTER **10**

The Eucharist

▶ **How might you react if Jesus visited your hometown?**

What would happen if Jesus made a personal appearance in your hometown? Naturally, the media would go into a frenzy. News organizations from all over the world would crowd into your hometown. The fact of the matter is that Jesus is always present in the world.

And behold, I am with you always, until the end of the age.

MATTHEW 28:20

▶ **Where and in whom do you experience the presence of Jesus?**

TIMELINE

| | 1999 Joint Declaration on Justification | 2009 Anglican Ordinariates begin to be established. | 2013 Inauguration Mass of Pope Francis |

| 1850 | 1900 | 1950 | 2000 | 2050 |

1871 Mass production of bread begins.　　2006 US FDA begins to regulate gluten-free products.

Alleviating Hunger

breadfor**the**world

HAVE FAITH. END HUNGER.

www.bread.org

Year after year, Bread members win far-reaching changes for hungry and poor people.

"Few can rival the voice and energy of Bread for the World."

– World Bank

In October 1972, a small group of Catholics and Protestants met to discuss and reflect on how persons of faith could have an impact on the problem of hunger in the world. They formed Bread for the World in order to do more than hand out food at the local food pantry, host a meal for the hungry, or take up an extra holiday collection to buy food for families. All of these actions are important, but more needed to be done. They talked and prayed about how they could tackle the problem of world hunger at its roots.

Today Bread for the World's 54,000 members work to eliminate the causes of hunger and poverty. They use the power they have as citizens. Some of their efforts include encouraging Congress to support relief efforts at home and abroad. Bread for the World is also striving to improve nutrition programs in schools and within communities.

In the past, Bread for the World has joined with the Catholic Church to seek meaningful, comprehensive debt relief in the hope to reduce hunger worldwide. This is an important solution because of the connection between poverty and hunger in countries around the world.

▶ How do you feed the hungry in the name of Jesus?

Alleviating Hunger

The members of Bread for the World believe that they can make this world a better place. They are serious in their efforts to follow Jesus' command to reach out to the thirsty and hungry in his name.

Recently, Bread for the World has co-produced a documentary that points to successes in alleviating hunger oversees through U.S. foreign aid assistance. This Christian organization supports innovation and effective solutions to severe hunger as a moral imperative. Especially during economic downturns, the world's most vulnerable people need our compassion. We as Christians are obligated to have a preferential option for the poor and

vulnerable. This is because Christ showed compassion to those who were the most vulnerable in society.

Bread for the World is a member of the Circle of Protection, a movement of religious leaders urging lawmakers to protect programs that are vital to hungry and poor people. This compassionate response echoes the prophets of the Old Testament who remind the people:

> See you lowly ones, and be glad;
> you who seek God, take heart!
>
> For the LORD hears the poor,
> does not spurn those in bondage.
>
> Let the heavens and the earth
> sing praise, the seas and whatever
> moves in them!
>
> PSALM 69:33–35

FAITH JOURNAL

What can you commit to doing with your parish or school to help alleviate hunger in your community?

▶ **FAITH FOCUS**

How is the Eucharist both a memorial and a sacrifice?

▶ **FAITH VOCABULARY**

Eucharist

memorial

sacrifice

Jesus told his disciples that when two or three gather in his name, he is there with them. He assured them:

"Again, . . . I say to you, if two of you agree on earth about anything for which they are to pray, it shall be granted to them by my heavenly Father. For where two or three are gathered together in my name, there am I in the midst of them." MATTHEW 18:19–20

Jesus is always present with the Church. He is present with us when we celebrate the Sacraments. He is present in a unique way when the Church celebrates the **Eucharist**.

As Sacrament

The Eucharist is the Sacrament of the Body and Blood of Christ. Jesus is uniquely and really present under the appearances of bread and wine. Through the words and actions of this Sacrament the bread and wine become the Body and Blood of Christ. We are made sharers in the Paschal Mystery. This is why we say the Eucharist is a Sacrament, a memorial, and a sacrifice.

Christ is truly human and truly divine. He knew and knows well the human need to come to know spiritual, or invisible, realities through visible and concrete signs. The Eucharist as Sacrament does just that. The Eucharist is the Sacrament in which we receive the Body and Blood of Christ.

As Memorial

The Church celebrates the Eucharist in response to Jesus' command,

"[D]o this in memory of me." LUKE 22:19

Sacrificial SACRAMENT

The Eucharist is a **memorial** of Christ's Paschal Mystery. The Eucharist does more than just recall or remember Jesus and his work. It makes Jesus really, truly, and substantially present with us. The Sacrament of the Eucharist makes it possible for us to take part in and share in the saving work of his Salvation, his Paschal Mystery. Another way of saying this is: The Eucharist gives us grace.

The Church uses the Greek word for memory, *anamnesis*, to capture this mystery of faith. At Mass we are with Christ, who is alive! Time and space are transcended. We are really sharing in the Paschal Mystery here and now!

As Sacrifice

At the Last Supper Jesus instituted the Eucharist. Joining with his disciples, Jesus ate the Passover meal with them. At the meal he did what they had always done—he blessed God, then took, broke, and shared bread with them. He next took and gave them a cup of wine to drink from. At the Last Supper Jesus gave those actions new meaning.

He said:

"This is my body, which will be given for you; do this in memory of me. . . . This cup is the new covenant in my blood, which will be shed for you." LUKE 22:19–20

Jesus was linking this Passover supper with his **sacrifice** on the Cross. The altar is a symbol of the sacrifice of Christ. Each celebration of the Eucharist is not a "new" sacrifice. It is a moment when we enter into and share in the timeless offering of the one sacrifice of Jesus Christ. Joined to Christ, the faithful become a living offering to God. On the Cross, Jesus offered himself to the Father once and for all time. The Eucharist as a sacrifice makes present again the sacrifice of Jesus on the Cross.

Although Jesus truly died on the Cross and was buried, he was raised from the dead to a new and glorified life. He ascended to the Father, where he lives in glory. He continues his saving work in the world through the Church, which Saint Peter the Apostle describes as a priestly people (see 1 Peter 2:9).

Jesus' priestly work did not come to an end when he returned to his Father. Jesus, our eternal High Priest, continues to offer through the Church his sacrifice to the Father and to intercede for us, his people.

▶ When have you experienced the presence of Christ in the Eucharist?

DID YOU KNOW?

There are other names the Church uses to describe the Eucharist: the Lord's Supper, the Holy Sacrifice, the Sacrifice of Praise, Holy Communion, and Holy Mass. Each name helps us understand some aspect of this awesome mystery of faith.

Faith CONNECTION

Describe to a friend which actions or words during the Eucharistic Prayer of the Mass help you understand the Eucharist as a sacrifice.

Celebrating the Eucharist

The Eucharist is "the source and summit of the Christian life" (*Constitution on the Church* 11). The heart of the Church, Christ himself, is found in the Eucharist. The Eucharistic celebration always includes certain elements that constitute one single act of worship.

Christ, the ageless and perpetual High Priest, offers the Eucharistic sacrifice. The same Christ, who is really and truly present with us under the appearances of bread and wine, is offering the sacrifice. He gives and is given. By virtue of their ordination, priests, such as your parish priest, act in the person of Christ when they celebrate the Eucharist. The Sacrament of Holy Orders consecrates or sets them apart for this unique ministry.

Liturgy of the Word

Taken from the Old Testament and the New Testament, the Word of God is proclaimed during every celebration of the Eucharist. By means of these Scripture readings, as well as the homily and the Prayer of the Faithful, we receive and respond to the Word of God.

Liturgy of the Eucharist

The Eucharistic presence of Christ is accomplished when the elements of wheat bread and grape wine, the matter of the Sacrament, are consecrated by a validly ordained priest. The consecration takes place during the Eucharistic Prayer. The celebrant-priest asks the Father to send the Holy Spirit so that our offerings may become the Body and Blood of Christ. He prays:

Make holy, therefore, these gifts we pray,

by sending down your Spirit upon them like the dewfall,

so that they may become for us the Body and Blood of our Lord Jesus Christ.

FROM ROMAN MISSAL,
EUCHARISTIC PRAYER II

Acting through the power of the Holy Spirit and in the name and the Person of Jesus, the priest continues. First taking the bread and then the wine, he says and does what Jesus did and said at the Last Supper.

▶ How do you prepare yourself to receive Holy Communion?

Surpassing Every Thought

Christ's Body and Blood, his soul and divinity, the whole Person of Christ becomes truly and substantially present under the physical appearances of bread and wine. Saint John Damascene (ca. 675–ca. 749) summarized this great mystery of our faith. He wrote:

> You ask how the bread becomes the Body of Christ, and the wine . . . the Blood of Christ. I shall tell you: the Holy Spirit comes upon them and accomplishes what surpasses every . . . thought.
>
> FROM ON THE TRUE FAITH

We participate in the Eucharist most fully when we receive Christ's Body and Blood in Holy Communion. The Church recommends that we receive Holy Communion whenever we take part in the Mass and are rightly disposed, that is, we are unaware of any mortal sins in our lives.

We are obliged to receive Holy Communion at least once a year. The Church also encourages us to receive Christ under the forms of bread and wine. However, if we receive under only one form, we still receive Christ whole and entire.

The Blessed Sacrament is another name for the Eucharist. The Blessed Sacrament is reserved in the tabernacle. It is reserved to be brought to the faithful who are unable to take part in the celebration of Mass and for the devotion of the people. In many parishes, lay people serve as extraordinary ministers of Holy Communion. In this ministry, they take the consecrated host to those who are sick or infirm and cannot get to church for Mass.

The Graces of the Eucharist

By partaking of the Eucharist, we take part in Christ's friendship with us in many ways.

One with Christ. In the Eucharist Christ comes to us. Joined to Christ in Baptism, we are strengthened in our union with Christ. The Eucharist nourishes the unity in the Body of Christ.

Spiritual food. The Eucharist is spiritual food. Sharing the Eucharist preserves, increases, and renews the Holy Spirit's life of grace within us. We are nourished through our communion with God and with one another.

Strength. Communion with Christ strengthens our ability to love and be loved. By frequently and regularly receiving the Eucharist, we are less inclined to give in to temptation and sin. The closer we stay to Christ and abide in his friendship, the less we want to abandon that friendship and the more of God's grace we are able to receive.

Forgiveness. Receiving Holy Communion cleanses us from all sin except mortal sin. If we are aware of having committed mortal sin, we must return to God's love and friendship in the Sacrament of Penance and Reconciliation before receiving Holy Communion.

Commitment to the poor. Shortly after calling his disciples friends, Jesus commanded them to "love one another" (John 15:17). If we receive the Bread of Life, but ignore those who need the bread of food to live, we dishonor Christ's friendship.

Everlasting friendship. The Eucharist is Christ's pledge of his friendship in this world and forever in the next. He promises that one day all those who are faithful to God will see him and share in his glory.

Faith helps us see that God's Revelation in the Old Covenant and in the New Covenant is one plan. At the Last Supper Jesus transformed the Passover meal into a memorial of his Death and Resurrection. The Eucharist became the new Passover meal. Through the transforming power of the Holy Spirit, the faithful become a living offering to God the Father. Joined to Christ and in unity with the Holy Spirit, we bless and give thanks to God the Father for his loving plan of creation and Salvation.

GRATITUDE in ACTION

Giving thanks to God is at the heart of the Eucharist.
During the celebration of the Eucharist, we join with Christ in giving thanks and praise to God the Father. We give thanks and praise to the Father for all the blessings we have received and continue to receive through Christ his Son.

Giving thanks through service puts the attitude of gratitude into action. Your attitude greatly influences the way you look at and respond to the world. Your attitude affects your behavior and the choices you make.

The truth is that, whether you are young or old, you need to be in touch with your attitude. You need to look at what is going on in your life, and at times make an attitude adjustment. You can avoid feeling sorry for yourself or being envious of others who seem to have more than you. By developing an attitude of gratitude you begin to recognize the many blessings and good things God has provided.

RADIANT WITH JOY

When you begin to see what you have and who you are, you express your gratitude to God for your life, your health, and other gifts. Some people, before they go to bed each night, write in their journal a list of things or events that happened that day for which they are grateful.

Look to God that you may be radiant with joy and your faces may not blush for shame.

PSALM 34:6

When you give glory to God, you will come to appreciate and value that you are blessed. You will rest better and arise in the morning ready to greet another new day.

▶ **Complete an acrostic poem using the word gratitude.**

_____
_____
_____
_____
_____
_____
_____
_____
_____
_____
_____
_____

MY FAITH CHOICE

This week I will choose to have an attitude of gratitude. I will:

_____
_____.

PRAY Lord Jesus, you have sacrificed your life for the Salvation of the world. Help me to show compassion for others in need and to have an attitude of gratitude. Amen.

Recall

Define each of these faith terms:

1. Eucharist _____

2. memorial _____

3. sacrifice _____

Choose one of the questions below and write a brief paragraph to answer your choice.

4. Explain what is meant by the Real Presence of Christ in the Eucharist.

_____

_____

5. Explain how the Eucharist strengthens our relationship with God and with one another.

_____

_____

Reflect

Using what you have learned in this chapter, reflect on and describe in your own words the meaning of this statement:

> *How holy this feast in which Christ is our food: his passion is recalled, grace fills our hearts, and we receive a pledge of the glory to come.*
>
> SAINT THOMAS AQUINAS

_____

_____

Share

Share with a friend examples of how to express an attitude of gratitude.

WITH MY FAMILY

Discuss with your family: In what ways does sharing in the Eucharist strengthen the unity of our family?

To Help You REMEMBER

1. The Mass is our celebration of thanksgiving to God for all he has done for us.

2. The Eucharist is the source and summit of the Church's life.

3. Holy Communion is our spiritual nourishment, helping us to have compassion and gratitude.

CHRIST with US

All: "[B]ehold, I am with you always, until the end of the age."

MATTHEW 28:20

Group 1: Christ with me, Christ before me,

Group 2: Christ behind me, Christ in me,

Group 1: Christ beneath me, Christ above me,

Group 2: Christ on my right, Christ on my left,

Group 1: Christ in my breadth, Christ in my length, Christ in my height, Christ in the mouth of everyone who speaks to me,

Group 2: Christ in the heart of everyone who thinks of me,

Group 1: Christ in every eye that sees me,

Group 2: Christ in every ear that hears me.

All: "[B]ehold, I am with you always, until the end of the age."

MATTHEW 28:20

BASED ON PRAYER OF SAINT PATRICK

LOOKING AHEAD
In this chapter the Holy Spirit invites you to ▶

EXPLORE stories of mercy and reconciliation.
DISCOVER the meaning of the Sacraments of Healing.
DECIDE how to share in Jesus' healing ministry.

CHAPTER **11**

Sacraments of HEALING

▶ What suffering in the world today concerns you most?

God knows the suffering that is going on in our world. Jesus himself personally suffered. He also reached out to people who were suffering and touched their lives with God's healing touch.

Jesus stretched out his hand, touched him, and said, "I do will it. Be made clean." And the leprosy left him immediately. LUKE 5:13

▶ How does the Church reach out to those who are suffering?

TIMELINE

	1538–1584 Life of St. Charles Borromeo		1877 Hôtel-Dieu de Paris Hospital reconstructed.	2000 The Church's Day of Pardon
1500		1800	1850	2000
		1820–1910 Florence Nightingale, founder of nursing	1822–1895 Louis Pasteur, a founder of microbiology	

Reaching Out to Heal

Throughout the centuries disciples of Jesus continue to heal the world through remarkable acts of forgiveness and reconciliation.

Perpetua and Felicity were two heroic young women who chose to be martyred rather than to give up their faith in Christ. They lived in the great city of Carthage, in North Africa, at the end of the second century. Perpetua was well educated, a wife and mother. Felicity was a slave who was pregnant with her first child.

Perpetua and Felicity embraced the Christian faith and way of life. They were preparing for Baptism when Emperor Severus made it illegal to convert to Christianity. Perpetua, Felicity, and a number of other Christians were arrested. Perpetua and Felicity were baptized shortly after they were condemned to death.

On the day of their execution, Perpetua and Felicity were led in front of violent animals and thrown to the ground, but the animals did not kill them. Gladiators then attempted to cut Perpetua's and Felicity's throats with a sword. The soldier who attacked Perpetua was inexperienced and hesitated to perform such a cruel act.

Perpetua, knowing that her death was inevitable and that this soldier would be severely punished for failing to carry out the emperor's command, took the young soldier's trembling hand and helped him meet his target. Perpetua's ability to think of the need of her attacker before her own life is an expression of love and mercy that echoes through the ages of Church history. The Church honors Saints Perpetua and Felicity on March 7.

▶ Have you ever made friends with someone who you thought was your enemy?

Returning Catholics

Some Catholics find themselves in spiritual darkness. For one reason or another they have become inactive members of the Church. Often this happens when a member of the faithful perceives that he or she has been hurt by someone of the Church in some way, or is struggling with a teaching of the Church.

Following Jesus' call to show mercy and to seek reconciliation, the Church reaches out to Catholics who are not actively taking part in the life of the Church and invites them into conversion. Welcoming back returning Catholics is often part of a parish's hospitality ministry.

People participating in a hospitality ministry of the Catholic Church often become spiritual companions to those returning back to active parish life. Each of us needs someone to walk with us on our faith journeys. Spiritual companions lead each other to new beginnings, to a place of renewal. They help each other listen to the whisper of the Holy Spirit guiding their lives. Together they come to a renewed understanding of the Church. Spiritual companions help each other discover ways to live as faithful and forgiven children of the Father.

Reconciling with the Church is an example of how some people re-enter into a relationship with Jesus. Returning Catholics join once again in living their lives in Christ as faithful members of the Church.

FAITH JOURNAL

When did you have the hardest time forgiving someone? Why?

▶ **FAITH FOCUS**

How is the Church a sign and instrument of Christ's healing?

▶ **FAITH VOCABULARY**

conversion

free will

seal of confession

Endure Suffering

Suffering, whether it is physical, emotional, or spiritual, can bring us to our knees. We may feel vulnerable and powerless. During such times, we often find ourselves turning to God and placing our hope and trust in him.

The Catholic Church continues Jesus' ministry of reaching out to people who suffer through the Sacraments of Healing—Anointing of the Sick and Penance and Reconciliation. The Church is a sign and instrument of Jesus' healing. Through the power of the Holy Spirit the Church continues that work until the end of time, when Christ will return in glory.

Anointing of the Sick

Jesus' compassion and ministry with the sick and dying are made present in the Church through the Sacrament of the Anointing of the Sick (read Matthew 9:35; James 5:13–14). This Sacrament confers the grace of strengthening our faith and trust in God. We receive the grace to face our sickness, weakness, or dying with courage and hope.

GOD'S HEALING LOVE

Celebrating the Sacrament

The Church celebrates the Anointing of the Sick with the faithful of all ages who are seriously ill or weak. Only bishops and priests can administer this Sacrament. The ritual for celebrating the Anointing of the Sick is simple. The principal elements of the rite are:

- the invocation of the Holy Spirit effected by the priest's silent laying on of hands,

- the prayers of intercession, and

- the anointing on the forehead and hands of the sick person with the blessed Oil of the Sick.

The Anointing of the Sick can be received each time a Christian falls seriously ill. It can also be celebrated more than once during the same illness if that illness worsens.

▶ What is the greatest need for healing that you have experienced?

Effects of the Sacrament

Anointing of the Sick, like each of the Sacraments, confers special graces. Some of the graces of this Sacrament are:

- God assures the grace of peace and courage to strengthen individuals to overcome any difficulties associated with serious illness and old age.

- This Sacrament provides healing for the soul and sometimes healing for the body.

- This Sacrament grants forgiveness of sins if the sick person is unable to receive forgiveness through the celebration of the Sacrament of Penance and Reconciliation.

- This Sacrament unites the sick person more closely to Christ's Passion. The person's suffering becomes a participation in Jesus' saving work.

- In cases when death is imminent, this Sacrament prepares the person for the final journey into eternal life.

If you have ever been seriously ill, you may have realized more deeply the importance of your relationship with Jesus. Celebrating the Anointing of the Sick strengthens your faith and can help you realize that God is present during your times of illness and weakness.

DID YOU KNOW?

One way that the Church ministers to the sick is through the establishment and staffing of hospitals. The word *hospital* comes from two Latin words meaning "house for guests."

The first Christian hospitals cared for weary travelers and people who were too sick to be cared for at home. The Hôtel Dieu in Paris, founded in the 600s, is the oldest Christian hospital still in existence.

Faith CONNECTION

Design a card for someone who is sick. Decorate it with a Scripture passage, for example, Psalm 23:1, Psalm 41:4, or Psalm 46:2, and a message of your own.

Against God's Will

God has gifted each one of us with **free will**. This gift refers to the ability that each and every human being has in choosing to follow God's will. A person's free will enables he or she to enter into a loving relationship with God and others.

Of course in any situation God's will for us is always what is good, true, and beautiful. God desires for us what is in our best interests and that which will lead us to eternal happiness. However human beings do not always trust God and do not discern right and wrong properly. As a result, we sometimes knowingly choose to go against God's will and commit sin.

The Sacrament of Penance

There is another kind of healing that all of us need because of our sins. It is the spiritual healing that is bestowed upon us through the Sacrament of Penance and Reconciliation. Each time we sin, the Holy Spirit calls us back to friendship with God and his people, the Church. We call this movement of turning our heart back to God's love **conversion**.

Jesus gave his Church the authority to forgive sins (see John 20:21–23; Matthew 16:19). When we sin after being baptized, we have the opportunity to have our broken friendship with God and the Church healed through celebrating the Sacrament of Penance and Reconciliation.

Reconciliation is the Sacrament through which we receive forgiveness of those sins we have

committed after Baptism. By the sincere confessing of one's sins to a priest, he forgive that person of his or her sins. There are four essential elements to the proper celebration of this Sacrament. They are contrition, confession, satisfaction, and absolution.

▶ When do you find it most difficult to trust God?

Contrition

Contrition is true sorrow for sins arising from our faith in God and love for him. True sorrow includes the desire not to sin again. Sorrow arising from love for God is called *perfect contrition*. Sorrow arising from other motives, such as the trouble sin has caused or the fear of discovery or the fear of punishment, is called *imperfect contrition*.

Confession

Confession is stating one's sins to a bishop or priest who, by his ordination, has the power to forgive sins in the name of Jesus Christ. We must confess all mortal sins we have not yet confessed. Church law requires us to confess our mortal sins at least once a year. The confession of venial sins,

while not necessary, is still highly recommended by the Church.

If you have any worries that the priest will tell others about your sins, put your fears to rest. Priests are under the **seal of confession.** This means that priests are bound to keep absolute secrecy regarding all sins confessed to them.

Satisfaction

Satisfaction means making up for our sins. We make satisfaction by accepting and performing the penance the priest assigns us. We have an obligation and responsibility to make reparation for our sins. Performing penance helps repair the harm caused by our sins. Penance also helps us develop good habits to live as disciples of Christ.

Absolution

Absolution is God's forgiving of sins by pardoning the wrongdoing of the one who has confessed his or her sins with a contrite heart. The words of absolution make clear that the power to forgive sins is God's alone, celebrated in the Church's ministry of healing.

▶ Why is imaking reparation for one's sins important?

Christ Hugging People, Nip Rogers

Effects of Penance and Reconciliation

The Sacrament of Penance and Reconciliation, like the other Sacraments, has its own special effects, or graces. Some of the graces of this Sacrament are:

- Penance and Reconciliation restores us to the loving relationship with God that we entered into at Baptism.

- This Sacrament restores us and heals any wounds we inflicted on the Church.

- Celebrating Penance and Reconciliation remits, or takes away, the spiritual consequences of mortal sin.

- This Sacrament strengthens our love for God and our relationship with him.

- Celebrating Penance and Reconciliation accomplishes the remission of temporal, or temporary, punishment either in part or entirely.

- We receive the spiritual strength to live faithfully as children of God, knowing that we have received his peace and mercy.

Forgive like God

The Sacraments of Healing are part of the foundation for living a Christian life. Jesus practiced a lifetime of forgiveness. Through God's love we are called to forgiveness, conversion, and healing. God asks us to forgive one another as he forgives us.

Some people think forgiving is easy. They say things like "Forgive and forget" and "Time heals all wounds." Other people believe if we just ignore the hurt, it will go away. Some want to get even or seek revenge. Jesus knew that forgiveness is very difficult for us. Jesus shows us how to forgive by the way he forgave (read Matthew 6:14–15; 18:21–22; Luke 23:24).

Holding on to hurt or grudges is painful. It drains your energy, your happiness, your spontaneity, and your dreams. We need to know how to forgive and how to receive forgiveness. Forgiveness is not necessarily:

- saying it is okay that the other person hurt you.
- forgetting about the hurt or harm.
- punishing the other person, or getting even.

STEPS TO SPIRITUAL HEALING

Jesus lived a lifetime of forgiveness. Here are some steps to help you live a life of forgiveness and healing:

- Pray and ask the Holy Spirit to open your mind and heart to forgive.
- Name the hurt, or whatever the person did to you. Talk to the person who hurt you. If that is not possible, talk to a trusted friend or parent, or write about how you feel. Expressing your feelings can help diminish the pain.
- Make a choice, a real decision, to forgive. Forgive is a verb, an action word. To forgive another is something you do.
- Forgiving is the best gift you can give yourself. It is what Jesus asks you to do, and it will lead to your own healing.

MY FAITH CHOICE

This week I will incorporate the steps to spiritual healing. I will:

_____

_____ .

 PRAY Holy Spirit, help heal my heart for this hurt [name hurt] so I can move on to feeling loved and loving others. Amen.

Recall

Define each of these faith terms:

1. conversion _____

2. free will _____

3. seal of confession _____

Choose one of the questions below and write a brief paragraph to answer your choice.

4. Describe the Rite of the Anointing of the Sick, then explain the effects of the sacramental grace.

_____

_____

5. Describe the Rite of Penance, then explain the effects of the sacramental grace.

_____

_____

To Help You REMEMBER

1. The Sacraments of Healing are Anointing of the Sick and Penance and Reconciliation.

2. The Church reaches out to all who are suffering with illness and the effects of old age through the Anointing of the Sick.

3. Each of us can experience God's healing grace in the Sacrament of Penance and Reconciliation.

Reflect

Using what you have learned in this chapter, reflect on and describe in your own words the meaning of this statement:

Today too, amid so much darkness, we need to see the light of hope and to be men and women who bring hope to others... [T]o look upon them with tenderness and love, Is to open up a horizon of hope; it is to let a shaft of light break through the heavy clouds; it is to bring the warmth of hope!

POPE FRANCIS, HOMILY, MARCH 19, 2013

_____

_____

Share

With a friend share an experience of receiving forgiveness and healing.

WITH MY FAMILY

Discuss as a family: How can we help to heal the hurt we may have caused to one another?

The JESUS Prayer

Jesus taught that we do not need to use many words when we pray. God knows what is in our hearts and on our minds before we share our feelings and thoughts with him. The Jesus Prayer is a simple form of prayer based on the Gospel story of Jesus healing the man born blind that uses few words.

Leader: Saint Paul encourages us to pray often. He wrote: "Pray without ceasing" (1 Thessalonians 5:17). Quietly pray the words "Jesus, Son of the living God, have mercy on me, a sinner" (based on Luke 18:38).

All: *Close your eyes, take a deep breath, and say the name, "Jesus, Son of the living God." Next pause briefly, exhale, and say, "have mercy on me, a sinner." Repeat the prayer slowly several times.*

LOOKING AHEAD
In this chapter the Holy
Spirit invites you to ▶

EXPLORE how a married couple serves.
DISCOVER which Sacraments celebrate a call to service.
DECIDE how to respond to your call to serve others.

CHAPTER **12**

▶ How do you see people serving one another?

Have you ever asked yourself, "What does God want from me?" Christians find the answers to that question in Jesus Christ. At the Last Supper, Jesus wrapped a towel around his waist and washed his disciples' feet. Making sure that no one missed the real meaning of what he was doing, Jesus said,

I have given you a model to follow, so that as I have done for you, you should also do. JOHN 13:15

▶ How does the Church serve others as Jesus taught?

Sacraments of Service

TIMELINE

1980 Pope John Paul II's pastoral provision for former Episcopal priests.

1981 LAMP Ministries begins.

1983 Most states have a "no-fault" divorce law.

1996 DOMA is enacted in the US.

2009 USCCB's *Marriage: Love and Life in the Divine Plan*

1980　1990　2000　2010

AN INSPIRING COUPLE

When Tom and Lynn first founded LAMP Ministries, the idea of "lay missionaries" was a strange term to many Catholics. Missionaries who went out into the world to evangelize were usually priests or religious sisters and brothers.

This married couple was inspired by the words of Pope Paul VI in his apostolic exhortation, *On Evangelization in the Modern World*. In this papal document the Pope reinforced the Church's teaching to evangelize all people. In 1981, with the blessing of the local bishop, Lay Apostolic Ministries with the Poor (LAMP) was born.

LAMP seeks to serve the spiritual needs of the materially poor through evangelization. The group serves people caught in the grip of drug addiction, violence, homelessness and despair. Through its services, the lives of many are touched and transformed.

In the late 1980s, LAMP rolled out the "LAMP café," a canteen truck out of which they provide physical and spiritual nourishment to people who are homeless. LAMP missionaries also witness to the dignity of human life in crisis pregnancy centers, and offer free retreats at the LAMP Prayer House for the Poor.

In recognition of their dedication to the material poor of New York City, LAMP received official canonical recognition from the Catholic Church through Cardinal John O'Connor of the Archdiocese of New York.

Giving Witness

Tom and Lynn have always felt the call to Christian service. Their vision for LAMP Ministries came about in a unique way through their sacramental union as husband and wife.

"Together, we arrived at the concept that we should do this work as a couple," Tom said. "We not only believe marriage is not an obstacle to many forms of non-ordained ministry, but through our efforts and struggles, we hope we have given witness to some of the possibilities that exist."

Tom and Lynn have been blessed with three children. They helped their parents see the poor through their eyes, and inspired the creation of the "lamplighters," a component of LAMP Ministries geared to children. Young lamplighters make art and craft projects that LAMP missionaries share with poor families.

Through over 30 years of ministry the leadership of LAMP have come to realize that they are a movement of the laity within the Church. LAMP leadership finds inspiration from the Sacred Heart of Jesus, directing what they do and how they love.

FAITH JOURNAL

How are you being called to serve others at this time in your life?

▶ **FAITH FOCUS**

How do Matrimony and Holy Orders serve the mission of the Church?

▶ **FAITH VOCABULARY**

celibacy

conjugal act

Set Aside

Christians are called to serve others as Jesus did. The Holy Spirit invites some members of the Church to living a life of service in a unique way. These people are consecrated, or set aside, for this holy work in the two Sacraments at the Service of Communion—Holy Orders and Matrimony.

Marriage

From the very beginning God created man and woman to be partners, sharing lives in faithful love (read Genesis 2:24). Marriage is a covenantal and permanent relationship between a man and a woman who are to love faithfully and exclusively, and be open to the gift of children. God himself endowed the natural institution of marriage with a number of essential qualities.

A covenant. Marriage is a relationship of love that a man and a woman freely and knowingly enter into with each other. A married couple becomes a living sign of the Covenant. As they grow together in love for one another, they are to love as God loves.

Permanent, or indissoluble. God's Covenant with his people is permanent. It is unbreakable, or indissoluble, and permanent by its very nature. So too marriage is to be between husband and wife.

Called to Serve the CHURCH

Faithful and exclusive. The marriage covenant is to be a lifelong relationship. This requires faithfulness and exclusivity on the part of married spouses. Therefore polygamy and adultery are contrary to these essential qualities of marriage. Polygamy is having more than one spouse at the same time. When a married person has sexual relations with another person, he or she commits adultery. Any non-marital sexual intercourse is a violation of the faithfulness and exclusivity necessary for marriage.

Openness to children. The willingness of a married couple to receive God's "supreme gift" of a child is at the heart of marital love (read Genesis 1:28). Married couples are to responsibly plan the growth and development of their family life. Any form of contraception is contrary to this essential quality of marriage. The Church encourages married couples to use Natural Family Planning as the way to responsibly plan the needs of the family, and honor the dignity of the **conjugal act**, and respect the female body.

▶ Why is marriage to be a covenantal relationship?

A Sign of God's Love

The Sacrament of Matrimony celebrates the marriage between a baptized man and a baptized woman. This Sacrament consecrates and strengthens the married couple to live as a sign of unity and love. They are called and receive the grace to be a mirror of God's love for us and of Christ's love for his Church. Matrimony gives the spouses the grace to love each other with the love with which Christ loves his Church.

The essential element of this Sacrament is the couple's exchange of marriage promises. The woman and man themselves are the ministers of this Sacrament. The priest or deacon receives the consent of the couple on behalf of the whole Church and gives the married couple the Church's blessing. Since Matrimony consecrates the couple to openly and publicly serve the whole Church, this Sacrament is appropriately celebrated at Mass in the presence of the worshiping assembly, which has gathered for the celebration.

The Priesthood of Christ

The whole Church is a priestly people. Through Baptism all believers are joined to Christ and are anointed to share in his priestly work. This participation in Christ's priesthood is called the common priesthood of the faithful.

Some members of the Church share in the priestly work of Christ in a unique way. They are members of the ministerial, or ordained, priesthood. The Sacrament of Holy Orders confers the ministerial priesthood upon those men called by God to serve the Church in this way. The ordained share in the priesthood of Christ in a way that differs in essence from the common priesthood of the faithful. The ordained continue the work Christ handed on to his Apostles. This ministry and office of the Church is ordered to serve the common priesthood of the faithful. The ministerial priesthood possesses a sacred power, which reaches its highest expression in the celebration of the Eucharist.

In Holy Orders a baptized man becomes a member of the order of bishops, priests, or deacons. The ministries imparted by Holy Orders are indispensable for the essential makeup of the Church. The People of God require the graces of the Sacraments ministered by bishops, priests, and deacons, as well as the spiritual and moral guidance of ordained ministers. The ordained help the laity to fully live out the baptismal vocation to witness for Christ in the world.

Three Degrees

Only Church authority has the right and responsibility to call baptized men to receive the Sacrament of Holy Orders. Ultimately, however, Christ bestows the Sacrament. He does so through his bishops, who are the successors to the Apostles, and who receive the fullness of this Sacrament.

The Sacrament of Holy Orders is conferred in all three degrees by a bishop. This is done by the laying on of hands upon the man being ordained. Following that, a solemn prayer of consecration is given. This prayer asks God to grant the *ordinand*, or man being ordained, the graces of the Holy Spirit required for his ministry.

▶ How is the service of the clergy different from the service of the laity?

Rite of Ordination

For example, the bishop at the ordination of a priest prays:

Almighty Father,
grant to these servants of yours
the dignity of the priesthood.
Renew within them the Spirit of holiness.
As co-workers with the order of bishops
may they be faithful to the ministry
that they receive from you, Lord God,
and be to others a model of right conduct.

May they be faithful in working with the order
of bishops,
so that the words of the Gospel may reach the ends
of the earth,
and the family of nations,
made one in Christ,
may become God's one, holy people.

FROM PRAYER OF CONSECRATION, *RITE OF ORDINATION* 26

Like those who receive Baptism and Confirmation, the ordinand is imprinted with an indelible sacramental seal. Whether the priest, bishop, or deacon is worthy or unworthy, Christ still acts through him. All the Sacraments he celebrates are valid because it is Christ who effects them. Christ is our one and only Priest, who is forever the one Mediator between God and us.

Faith CONNECTION

What does it mean to say that a priest shares in the one priesthood of Jesus Christ?

Bishop

A bishop receives the fullness of Holy Orders. Bishops are successors to the Apostles and share in the responsibility of the service Christ gave to his Apostles. Appointed by the Pope, the bishop is the visible head of a particular Church entrusted to his care.

The Pope is the bishop of Rome, and in this capacity serves as the universal shepherd of the Catholic Church. Each Pope selects his own unique motto, which gives focus to his papacy.

▶ What is the motto of your bishop?

Priests

Priests in the Roman Catholic Church give themselves entirely to God and to the service of the Church. This is exemplified by their disciplinary vow of **celibacy**. To be celibate means not to marry. Together with the bishop, priests form the *presbyterium*, or council of priests. They serve the people of the particular Church the bishop serves as leader.

Priests are dependent upon the bishops for the exercise of their ministries of proclaiming and preaching the Word of God, leading the faithful in worship, and guiding the faithful in living the Gospel. Priests receive their assignments from bishops and not from the people of the parishes they serve.

Deacons

Deacons carry out their work of service under the pastoral authority of the bishop. They assist bishops and priests at the celebration of Mass, in the distribution of Holy Communion, in blessing marriages, in the proclamation of the Gospel, in preaching, and in dedicating themselves to works of loving service. Married men may be ordained to the order of the permanent diaconate.

LOVE BEGINS at HOME

The family is a sign of God's love. Within our families, we first learn the meaning of love and service. Children first hear God's invitation to love without limits in the experience of being loved by their parents or guardians and seeing the love a husband and a wife have for one another.

The Christian family is "a community of grace and prayer, a school of human virtues and of Christian charity" (*Catechism of the Catholic Church* 1666). For this reason the Christian family is called a "domestic Church."

Love is the foundation of civilization. The Christian family is the first source of that love for its members. Sharing that love in word and action, one day at a time, helps prepare for the coming of the Kingdom of God (read John 13:34–35).

▶ In which ways is your family a sign of God's love?

WORKS OF MERCY

Living the Works of Mercy enables you to reach out in love and service to your family and friends, and to your neighbors and to people all over the world. Identify the Work of Mercy described in each item in this list. Then answer the questions.

■ Your family feeds and nurtures you physically, spiritually, and emotionally. What can you do to nourish your family? How can you reach out to others beyond your family?

■ Your family comforts and cares for you when you are sick, sad, or hurting physically, spiritually, and emotionally. What can you do to comfort and care for your family? How can you reach out to others beyond your family?

■ Your family is patient with you and forgives you when you hurt them. How can you practice patience and forgiveness in return? How can you practice patience and forgiveness with people outside your family?

MY FAITH CHOICE

Choose one other Work of Mercy to put into practice this week. This week I will commit to loving and serving others by:

_____

_____ .

 PRAY Lord of Life, you are the source of love. Help me to love others and myself as you love. Guide me in Christian service. Amen.

Recall

Define each of these faith terms:

1. celibacy _____

2. conjugal act _____

3. consecrated _____

4. ordained _____

Write a brief paragraph to answer each question.

5. Identify and explain the essential qualities of marriage.

_____

_____

6. Describe the effects of the Sacrament of Matrimony upon the married couple.

_____

_____

7. Identify and explain the essential elements of the Rite of Ordination.

_____

_____

Reflect

Using what you have learned in this chapter, reflect on and describe in your own words the meaning of this statement:

Love is now no longer a mere "command"; it is the response to the gift of love with which God draws near to us.

POPE BENEDICT XVI, *GOD IS LOVE*, INTRODUCTION

_____

_____

Share

With a partner share how you would explain God's unique plan for life and love in marriage.

WITH MY FAMILY

Discuss with your family: How does our family model loving acts of service?

To Help You REMEMBER

1. The Sacraments at the Service of Communion are Holy Orders and Matrimony.

2. The man and woman who celebrate the Sacrament of Matrimony become a living sign of God's fidelity.

3. Holy Orders consecrates men who are called to serve, teach, and lead members of the Church.

The BEATITUDES

The Beatitudes set before us the values and vision that are at the foundation of living the Gospel. They are the source of true happiness proclaimed and revealed in Jesus Christ.

Group 1: Blessed are the poor in spirit,

All: **for theirs is the kingdom of heaven.**

Group 2: Blessed are they who mourn,

All: **for they will be comforted.**

Group 1: Blessed are the meek,

All: **for they will inherit the land.**

Group 2: Blessed are they who hunger and thirst for righteousness,

All: **for they will be satisfied.**

Group 1: Blessed are the merciful,

All: **for they will be shown mercy.**

Group 2: Blessed are the clean of heart,

All: **for they will see God.**

Group 1: Blessed are the peacemakers,

All: **for they will be called children of God.**

Group 2: Blessed are they who are persecuted for the sake of righteousness,

All: **for theirs is the kingdom of heaven.**

(Share a sign of peace.)

BASED ON MATTHEW 5:3–10

Ⓐ Choose the Best Word

Answer each question by circling the best answer.

1. In 313 under which Roman Emperor did Christianity become the official religion of the Roman Empire?

   A. Charlemagne

   B. Domitian

   C. Constantine

   D. Caesar

2. Which are the Sacraments of Christian Initiation?

   A. Baptism, Confirmation, and the Eucharist

   B. Baptism, Eucharist, and Holy Orders

   C. Baptism, Holy Orders, and Matrimony

   D. Baptism, Eucharist, and Matrimony

3. Which of the following describes the Sacrament of the Eucharist?

   A. We receive the Body and Blood of Christ.

   B. Jesus is present under the appearance of bread and wine.

   C. We are joined with Christ and give praise and thanksgiving to the Father.

   D. all of the above

4. In the Sacrament of the Anointing of the Sick, we ___

   A. receive the grace to face illness with courage and strength.

   B. receive forgiveness of Original Sin.

   C. are anointed with blessed oil.

   D. both A and C

5. In the Sacraments at the Service of Communion ___

   A. a baptized man and a baptized woman become a sign of Christ's love for the Church.

   B. a baptized man is consecrated to serve the whole Church as a bishop, priest, or deacon.

   C. a bishop is elected Pope.

   D. both A and B

B Show What You Know

Match the item in Column A with those in Column B.

Column A

_____ **1.** Paschal Mystery

_____ **2.** grace

_____ **3.** liturgical year

_____ **4.** sacramental

_____ **5.** Blessed Sacrament

_____ **6.** manna

_____ **7.** conversion

_____ **8.** seal of confession

_____ **9.** priesthood of the faithful

_____ **10.** ministerial priesthood

Column B

A. gift from God that makes us sharers of divine life

B. sacred signs such as the altar, statues, and blessings

C. bread-like food that the Israelites ate during the Exodus

D. turning our hearts toward God

E. conferred by the sacrament of Holy Orders

F. cycle of seasons and feasts the Church celebrates

G. absolute secrecy binding priests regarding sins confessed to them

H. Jesus' Passion, Death, Resurrection, and Ascension

I. sharing by all the baptized in Christ's priestly ministry

J. the Eucharist reserved in the tabernacle

C Connect with Scripture

Reread the Scripture passage on the first Unit Opener page. What connection do you see between this passage and what you learned in this unit?

_____

_____

_____

D Be a Disciple

1. *Review The Church Follows Jesus in each of the chapters. Which person or ministry has inspired you to be a better disciple of Jesus? Explain your response.*

_____

_____

_____

2. *Work with a group. Review the six Disciple Power habits you have learned about in this unit. After jotting down your own ideas, share with the group practical ways that you will live these day by day.*

_____

_____

_____

CATHOLIC PRAYERS and PRACTICES

Sign of the Cross

In the name of the Father,
and of the Son,
and of the Holy Spirit. Amen.

Signum Crucis

In nómine Patris,
et Fílii,
et Spíritus Sancti. Amen.

Our Father

Our Father, who art in heaven,
hallowed be thy name;
thy kingdom come,
thy will be done
on earth as it is in heaven.
Give us this day our daily bread,
and forgive us our trespasses,
as we forgive those who trespass
    against us;
and lead us not into temptation
    but deliver us from evil.
Amen.

Pater Noster

Pater noster, qui es in cælis:
sanctificétur nomen tuum;
advéniat regnum tuum;
fiat volúntas tua, sicut in cælo,
    et in terra.
Panem nostrum cotidiánum
    da nobis hódie;
et dimítte nobis débita nostra,
sicut et nos dimíttimus
    debitóribus nostris;
et ne nos indúcas in tentatiónem;
sed líbera nos a malo. Amen.

Glory Be (Doxology)

Glory be to the Father
and to the Son
and to the Holy Spirit,
as it was in the beginning
is now, and ever shall be
world without end. Amen.

Gloria Patri

Glória Patri
et Fílio
et Spirítui Sancto.
Sicut erat in princípio,
et nunc et semper
et in sǽcula sæculórum. Amen.

The Hail Mary

Hail, Mary, full of grace,
the Lord is with thee.
Blessed art thou among women
and blessed is the fruit of thy
    womb, Jesus.
Holy Mary, Mother of God,
pray for us sinners,
now and at the hour of our death.
Amen.

Ave, Maria

Ave, María, grátia plena,
Dóminus tecum.
Benedícta tu in muliéribus,
et benedíctus fructus ventris tui, Iesus.
Sancta María, Mater Dei,
ora pro nobis peccatóribus,
nunc et in hora mortis nostræ.
Amen.

Apostles' Creed

(from the *Roman Missal*)

I believe in God,
the Father almighty,
Creator of heaven and earth,
and in Jesus Christ, his only Son, our Lord,

*(At the words that follow, up to and
including the Virgin Mary, all bow.)*

who was conceived by the Holy Spirit,
born of the Virgin Mary,
suffered under Pontius Pilate,
was crucified, died and was buried;
he descended into hell;
on the third day he rose again from the dead;
he ascended into heaven,
and is seated at the right hand of God the Father almighty;
from there he will come to judge the living and the dead.

I believe in the Holy Spirit,
the holy catholic Church,
the communion of saints,
the forgiveness of sins,
the resurrection of the body,
and life everlasting. Amen.

Nicene Creed

(from the *Roman Missal*)

I believe in one God,
the Father almighty,
maker of heaven and earth,
of all things visible and invisible.

I believe in one Lord Jesus Christ,
the Only Begotten Son of God,
born of the Father before all ages.
God from God, Light from Light,
true God from true God,
begotten, not made, consubstantial with the Father;
through him all things were made.
For us men and for our salvation
he came down from heaven,

*(At the words that follow, up to and
including and became man, all bow.)*

and by the Holy Spirit was incarnate of the Virgin Mary,
and became man.

For our sake he was crucified under Pontius Pilate,
he suffered death and was buried,
and rose again on the third day
in accordance with the Scriptures.
He ascended into heaven
and is seated at the right hand of the Father.
He will come again in glory
to judge the living and the dead
and his kingdom will have no end.

I believe in the Holy Spirit, the Lord, the giver of life,
who proceeds from the Father and the Son,
who with the Father and the Son is adored and glorified,
who has spoken through the prophets.

I believe in one, holy, catholic and apostolic Church.
I confess one Baptism for the forgiveness of sins
and I look forward to the resurrection of the dead
and the life of the world to come. Amen.

Morning Prayer

Dear God,
as I begin this day,
keep me in your love and care.
Help me to live as your child today.
Bless me, my family, and my friends
    in all we do.
Keep us all close to you. Amen.

Grace Before Meals

Bless us, O Lord,
and these thy gifts,
which we are about to receive
from thy bounty,
through Christ our Lord.
Amen.

Grace After Meals

We give thee thanks
for all thy benefits, almighty God,
who lives and reigns forever.
Amen.

Evening Prayer

Dear God,
I thank you for today.
Keep me safe throughout the night.
Thank you for all the good I did today.
I am sorry for what I have chosen
    to do wrong.
Bless my family and friends. Amen.

A Vocation Prayer

God, I know you will call me
for special work in my life.
Help me follow Jesus each day
and be ready to answer your call. Amen.

Prayer to the Holy Spirit

Come, Holy Spirit, fill the hearts
    of your faithful.
And kindle in them the
    fire of your love.
Send forth your Spirit and
    they shall be created.
And you will renew the
    face of the earth. Amen.

Act of Contrition

My God,
I am sorry for my sins
    with all my heart.
In choosing to do wrong
and failing to do good,
I have sinned against you
whom I should love above all things.
I firmly intend, with your help,
to do penance,
to sin no more,
and to avoid whatever leads me to sin.
Our Savior Jesus Christ
suffered and died for us.
In his name, my God, have mercy. Amen.

The Beatitudes

"Blessed are the poor in spirit,
   for theirs is the kingdom of heaven.
Blessed are they who mourn,
   for they will be comforted.
Blessed are the meek,
   for they will inherit the land.
Blessed are they who hunger
    and thirst for righteousness,
   for they will be satisfied.
Blessed are the merciful,
   for they will be shown mercy.
Blessed are the clean of heart,
   for they will see God.
Blessed are the peacemakers,
   for they will be called children of God.
Blessed are they who are persecuted for
    the sake of righteousness,
   for theirs is the kingdom of heaven."

Matthew 5:3–10

The Angelus

Leader: The Angel of the Lord declared unto Mary,

Response: And she conceived of the Holy Spirit.

All: **Hail, Mary . . .**

Leader: Behold the handmaid of the Lord,

Response: Be it done unto me according to your Word.

All: **Hail, Mary . . .**

Leader: And the Word was made flesh,

Response: And dwelt among us.

All: **Hail, Mary . . .**

Leader: Pray for us, O holy Mother of God,

Response: That we may be made worthy of the promises of Christ.

Leader: Let us pray. Pour forth, we beseech you, oh Lord, your grace into our hearts; that we, to whom the Incarnation of Christ your Son was made known by the message of an Angel, may by his Passion and Cross be brought to the glory of his Resurrection. Through the same Christ our Lord.

All: **Amen.**

The Ten Commandments

1. I am the LORD your God: you shall not have strange gods before me.

2. You shall not take the name of the LORD your God in vain.

3. Remember to keep holy the LORD's Day.

4. Honor your father and your mother.

5. You shall not kill.

6. You shall not commit adultery.

7. You shall not steal.

8. You shall not lie.

9. You shall not covet your neighbor's wife.

10. You shall not covet your neighbor's goods.

Based on Exodus 20:2–3, 7–17

Precepts of the Church

1. Participate In Mass on Sundays and holy days of obligation, and rest from unnecessary work.

2. Confess sins at least once a year.

3. Receive Holy Communion at least during the Easter season.

4. Observe the prescribed days of fasting and abstinence.

5. Provide for the material needs of the Church, according to one's abilities.

The Great Commandment

"You shall love the Lord, your God, with all your heart, with all your soul, and with all your mind. . . . You shall love your neighbor as yourself."

Matthew 22:37, 39

The Law of Love

"This is my commandment: love one another as I love you."

John 15:12

Corporal Works of Mercy

Feed people who are hungry.
Give drink to people who are thirsty.
Clothe people who need clothes.
Visit people who are in prison.
Shelter people who are homeless.
Visit people who are sick.
Bury people who have died.

Spiritual Works of Mercy

Help people who sin.
Teach people who are ignorant.
Give advice to people who have doubts.
Comfort people who suffer.
Be patient with other people.
Forgive people who hurt you.
Pray for people who are alive and for those who have died.

Rosary

Catholics pray the Rosary to honor Mary and remember the important events in the life of Jesus and Mary. There are twenty mysteries of the Rosary. Follow the steps from 1 to 5.

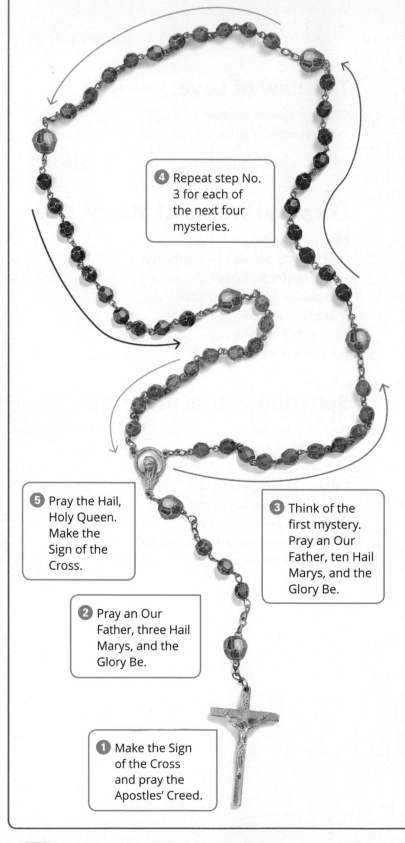

4 Repeat step No. 3 for each of the next four mysteries.

5 Pray the Hail, Holy Queen. Make the Sign of the Cross.

3 Think of the first mystery. Pray an Our Father, ten Hail Marys, and the Glory Be.

2 Pray an Our Father, three Hail Marys, and the Glory Be.

1 Make the Sign of the Cross and pray the Apostles' Creed.

Joyful Mysteries

1 The Annunciation
2 The Visitation
3 The Nativity
4 The Presentation in the Temple
5 The Finding of the Child Jesus after Three Days in the Temple

Luminous Mysteries

1 The Baptism at the Jordan
2 The Miracle at Cana
3 The Proclamation of the Kingdom and the Call to Conversion
4 The Transfiguration
5 The Institution of the Eucharist

Sorrowful Mysteries

1 The Agony in the Garden
2 The Scourging at the Pillar
3 The Crowning with Thorns
4 The Carrying of the Cross
5 The Crucifixion and Death

Glorious Mysteries

1 The Resurrection
2 The Ascension
3 The Descent of the Holy Spirit at Pentecost
4 The Assumption of Mary
5 The Crowning of the Blessed Virgin as Queen of Heaven and Earth

Hail, Holy Queen

Hail, holy Queen, Mother of mercy:
Hail, our life, our sweetness,
          and our hope.
To you do we cry, poor banished
          children of Eve.
To you do we send up our sighs,
mourning and weeping
          in this valley of tears.
Turn then, most gracious advocate,
your eyes of mercy toward us;
and after this our exile
show unto us the blessed fruit
          of your womb, Jesus.
O clement, O loving, O sweet
          Virgin Mary.

Stations of the Cross

1. Jesus is condemned to death.

2. Jesus accepts his cross.

3. Jesus falls the first time.

4. Jesus meets his mother.

5. Simon helps Jesus carry the cross.

6. Veronica wipes the face of Jesus.

7. Jesus falls the second time.

8. Jesus meets the women of Jerusalem.

9. Jesus falls the third time.

10. Jesus is stripped of his clothes.

11. Jesus is nailed to the cross.

12. Jesus dies on the cross.

13. Jesus is taken down from the cross.

14. Jesus is buried in the tomb.

(Some parishes conclude the Stations by reflecting on the Resurrection of Jesus.)

WE CELEBRATE the MASS

The Introductory Rites

We remember that we are the community of the Church.
We prepare to listen to the Word of God and to celebrate the Eucharist.

The Entrance

We stand as the priest, deacon, and other ministers enter the assembly. We sing a gathering song. The priest and deacon kiss the altar. The priest then goes to the chair where he presides over the celebration.

Greeting of the Altar and of the People Gathered

The priest leads us in praying the Sign of the Cross. The priest greets us, and we say,

"And with your spirit."

The Penitential Act

We admit our wrongdoings.
We bless God for his mercy.

The Gloria

We praise God for all the good that he has done for us.

The Collect

The priest leads us in praying the Collect. We respond, **"Amen."**

The Liturgy of the Word

God speaks to us today. We listen and respond to God's Word.

The First Reading from Scripture

We sit and listen as the lector reads from the Old Testament or from the Acts of the Apostles. The lector concludes, "The word of the Lord." We respond,

"Thanks be to God."

The Responsorial Psalm

The cantor leads us in singing a psalm.

The Second Reading from Scripture

The lector reads from the New Testament, but not from the four Gospels. The lector concludes, "The word of the Lord." We respond,

"Thanks be to God."

The Acclamation

We stand to honor Christ, present with us in the Gospel. The cantor leads us in singing **"Alleluia, Alleluia, Alleluia,"** or another acclamation during Lent.

The Gospel

The deacon or priest proclaims, "A reading from the holy Gospel according to (name of Gospel writer)." We respond,

"Glory to you, O Lord."

He proclaims the Gospel. At the end he says, "The Gospel of the Lord." We respond,

"Praise to you, Lord Jesus Christ."

The Homily

We sit. The priest or deacon preaches the homily. He helps the people gathered to understand the Word of God spoken to us in the readings.

The Profession of Faith

We stand and profess our faith.
We pray the Nicene Creed or the Apostles' Creed together.

The Prayer of the Faithful

The priest leads us in praying for our Church and her leaders, for our country and its leaders, for ourselves and others, for those who are sick and those who have died. We can respond to each prayer in several ways. One way that we respond is,

"Lord, hear our prayer."

The Liturgy of the Eucharist

We join with Jesus and the Holy Spirit to give thanks and praise to God the Father.

The Preparation of the Gifts

We sit as the altar is prepared and the collection is taken up. We share our blessings with the community of the Church and especially with those in need. The song leader may lead us in singing a song. The gifts of bread and wine are brought to the altar.

The priest lifts up the bread and blesses God for all our gifts. He prays, "Blessed are you, Lord God of all creation . . ." We respond,

"Blessed be God for ever."

The priest lifts up the cup of wine and prays, "Blessed are you, Lord God of all creation . . ."
We respond,

"Blessed be God for ever."

The priest invites us,
"Pray, brothers and sisters, that my sacrifice and yours may be acceptable to God, the almighty Father."

We stand and respond,

"May the Lord accept the sacrifice at your hands for the praise and glory of his name, for our good, and the good of all his holy Church."

The Prayer over the Offerings

The priest leads us in praying the Prayer over the Offerings.
We respond, **"Amen."**

Preface

The priest invites us to join in praying the Church's great prayer of praise and thanksgiving to God the Father.

Priest: "The Lord be with you."

Assembly: **"And with your spirit."**

Priest: "Lift up your hearts."

Assembly: **"We lift them up to the Lord."**

Priest: "Let us give thanks to the Lord our God."

Assembly: **"It is right and just."**

After the priest sings or prays aloud the Preface, we join in acclaiming,

**"Holy, Holy, Holy Lord God of hosts.
Heaven and earth are full of your glory.
Hosanna in the highest.
Blessed is he who comes in the name of
the Lord.
Hosanna in the highest."**

The Eucharistic Prayer

The priest leads the assembly in praying the Eucharistic Prayer. We call on the Holy Spirit to make our gifts of bread and wine holy and that they become the Body and Blood of Jesus. We recall what happened at the Last Supper. The bread and wine become the Body and Blood of the Lord. Jesus is truly and really present under the appearances of bread and wine.

The priest sings or says aloud, "The mystery of faith." We respond using this or another acclamation used by the Church,

> **"We proclaim your Death, O Lord, and profess your Resurrection until you come again."**

The priest then prays for the Church. He prays for the living and the dead.

Doxology

The priest concludes the praying of the Eucharistic Prayer. He sings or prays aloud,

> "Through him, and with him, and in him,
> O God, almighty Father,
> in the unity of the Holy Spirit,
> all glory and honor is yours,
> for ever and ever."

We respond by singing, **"Amen."**

The Communion Rite

The Lord's Prayer

We pray the Lord's Prayer together.

The Sign of Peace

The priest invites us to share a sign of peace, saying, "The peace of the Lord be with you always." We respond,

> **"And with your spirit."**

We share a sign of peace.

The Fraction, or the Breaking of the Bread

The priest breaks the host, the consecrated bread. We sing or pray aloud,

> **"Lamb of God, you take away
> the sins of the world,
> have mercy on us.
> Lamb of God, you take away
> the sins of the world,
> have mercy on us.
> Lamb of God, you take away
> the sins of the world,
> grant us peace."**

Communion

The priest raises the host and says aloud,

> "Behold the Lamb of God,
> behold him who takes away the sins
> of the world.
> Blessed are those called to the supper
> of the Lamb."
> We join with him and say,
>> **"Lord, I am not worthy
>> that you should enter under my roof,
>> but only say the word
>> and my soul shall be healed."**

The priest receives Communion. Next, the deacon and the extraordinary ministers of Holy Communion and the members of the assembly receive Communion.

The priest, deacon, or extraordinary minister of Holy Communion holds up the host. We bow, and the priest, deacon, or extraordinary minister of Holy Communion says, "The Body of Christ." We respond, **"Amen."** We then receive the consecrated host in our hands or on our tongues.

If we are to receive the Blood of Christ, the priest, deacon, or extraordinary minister of Holy Communion holds up the cup containing the consecrated wine. We bow, and the priest, deacon, or extraordinary minister of Holy Communion says, "The Blood of Christ." We respond, **"Amen."** We take the cup in our hands and drink from it.

The Prayer after Communion

We stand as the priest invites us to pray, saying, "Let us pray." He prays the Prayer after Communion. We respond,
"Amen."

The Concluding Rites

We are sent forth to do good works, praising and blessing the Lord.

Greeting

We stand. The priest greets us as we prepare to leave. He says, "The Lord be with you."
We respond,
 "And with your spirit."

Final Blessing

The priest or deacon may invite us,
 "Bow down for the blessing."

The priest blesses us, saying,
 "May almighty God bless you,
 the Father, and the Son,
 and the Holy Spirit."
We respond, **"Amen."**

Dismissal of the People

The priest or deacon sends us forth, using these or similar words,
 "Go in peace, glorifying the Lord
 by your life."
We respond,
 "Thanks be to God."
We sing a hymn. The priest and the deacon kiss the altar. The priest, deacon, and other ministers bow to the altar and leave in procession.

KEY TEACHINGS of the CHURCH

DIVINE REVELATION

Who am I?
Every human person has been created by God to live in friendship with him both here on Earth and forever in Heaven.

How do we know this about ourselves?
We know this because every human person desires to know and love God and wants God to know and love them. We also know this because God told us this about ourselves and about him.

How did God tell us?
First of all God tells us this through creation, which is the work of God; creation reflects the goodness and beauty of the Creator and tells us about God the Creator. Secondly, God came to us and told us, or revealed this about himself. He revealed this most fully by sending his Son, Jesus Christ, who became one of us and lived among us.

What is faith?
Faith is a supernatural gift from God that enables us to know God and all that he has revealed, and to respond to God with our whole heart and mind.

What is a mystery of faith?
The word *mystery* describes the fact that we can never fully comprehend or fully grasp God and his loving plan for us. We only know who God is and his plan for us through Divine Revelation.

What is Divine Revelation?
Divine Revelation is God's free gift of making himself known to us and giving himself to us by gradually communicating in deeds and words his own mystery and his divine plan for humanity. God reveals himself so that we can live in communion with him and with one another forever.

What is Sacred Tradition?
The word *tradition* comes from a Latin word meaning "to pass on." Sacred Tradition is the passing on of Divine Revelation by the Church through the power and guidance of the Holy Spirit.

What is the deposit of faith?
The deposit of faith is the source of faith that we draw from in order to pass on God's Revelation. The deposit of faith is the unity of Sacred Scripture and Sacred Tradition handed on by the Church from the time of the Apostles.

What is the Magisterium?
The Magisterium is the teaching authority of the Church. Guided by the Holy Spirit, the Church has the responsibility to authentically and accurately interpret the Word of God, both in Sacred Scripture and in Sacred Tradition. She does this to assure that her understanding of Revelation is faithful to the teaching of the Apostles.

What is a dogma of faith?
A dogma of faith is a truth taught by the Church as revealed by God and to which we are called to give our assent of mind and heart in faith.

SACRED SCRIPTURE

What is Sacred Scripture?
The words *sacred scripture* come from two Latin words meaning "holy writings." Sacred Scripture is the collection of all the writings God has inspired authors to write in his name.

What is the Bible?
The word *bible* comes from a Greek word meaning "book." The Bible is the collection of the forty-six books of the Old Testament and the twenty-seven books of the New Testament named by the Church as all the writings God has inspired human authors to write in his name.

What is the canon of Scripture?
The word *canon* comes from a Greek word meaning "measuring rod," or standard by which something is judged. The canon of Scripture is the list of books that the Church has identified and teaches to be the inspired Word of God.

What is biblical inspiration?
Biblical inspiration is a term that describes the Holy Spirit guiding the human authors of Sacred Scripture so that they faithfully and accurately communicate the Word of God.

What is the Old Testament?
The Old Testament is the first main part of the Bible. It is the forty-six books inspired by the Holy Spirit, written before the birth of Jesus and centered on the Covenant between God and his people, Israel, and the promise of the Messiah or Savior. The Old Testament is divided into the Torah/Pentateuch, historical books, wisdom literature, and writings of the prophets.

What is the Torah?
The Torah is the Law of God that was revealed to Moses. The written Torah is found in the first five books of the Old Testament, which are called the "Torah" or the "Pentateuch."

What is the Pentateuch?

The word *pentateuch* means "five containers." The Pentateuch is the first five books of the Old Testament, namely Genesis, Exodus, Leviticus, Numbers, and Deuteronomy.

What is the Covenant?

The Covenant is the solemn agreement of fidelity that God and his people freely entered into. It was renewed and fulfilled in Jesus Christ, the new and everlasting Covenant.

What are the historical books of the Old Testament?

The historical books tell about the fidelity and infidelity of God's people to the Covenant and about the consequences of those choices.

What are the Wisdom writings of the Old Testament?

The Wisdom writings are the seven books of the Old Testament that contain inspired practical advice and common-sense guidelines for living the Covenant and the Law of God. They are the Book of Job, Book of Psalms, Book of Ecclesiastes, Book of Wisdom, Book of Proverbs, Book of Sirach (Ecclesiasticus), and Song of Songs.

What are the writings of the prophets in the Old Testament?

The word *prophet* comes from a Greek word meaning "those who speak before others." The biblical prophets were those people God had chosen to speak in his name. The writings of the prophets are the eighteen books of the Old Testament that contain the message of the prophets to God's people. They remind God's people of his unending fidelity to them and of their responsibility to be faithful to the Covenant.

What is the New Testament?

The New Testament is the second main part of the Bible. It is the twenty-seven books inspired by the Holy Spirit and written in apostolic times that center on Jesus Christ and his saving work among us. The main parts are the four Gospels, the Acts of the Apostles, the twenty-one letters, and the Book of Revelation.

What are the Gospels?

The word *gospel* comes from a Greek word meaning "good news." The Gospel is the Good News of God's loving plan of Salvation, revealed in the Passion, Death, Resurrection, and Ascension of Jesus Christ. The Gospels are the four written accounts of Matthew, Mark, Luke, and John. The four Gospels occupy a central place in Sacred Scripture because Jesus Christ is their center.

What is an epistle?

The word *epistle* comes from a Greek word meaning "message or letter." An epistle is a formal type of letter. Some of the letters in the New Testament are epistles.

What are the Pauline Epistles and letters?

The Pauline Epistles and letters are the fourteen letters in the New Testament traditionally attributed to Saint Paul the Apostle.

What are the Catholic Letters?

The Catholic Letters are the seven New Testament letters that bear the names of the Apostles John, Peter, Jude, and James, and which were written to the universal Church rather than to a particular Church community.

THE HOLY TRINITY

Who is the Mystery of the Holy Trinity?

The Holy Trinity is the mystery of One God in Three Divine Persons—God the Father, God the Son, God the Holy Spirit. It is the central mystery of the Christian faith.

Who is God the Father?

God the Father is the First Person of the Holy Trinity.

Who is God the Son?

God the Son is Jesus Christ, the Second Person of the Holy Trinity. He is the Only Begotten Son of the Father who took on flesh and became one of us without giving up his divinity.

Who is God the Holy Spirit?

God the Holy Spirit is the Third Person of the Holy Trinity, who proceeds from the Father and Son. He is the Advocate, or Paraclete, sent to us by the Father in the name of his Son, Jesus.

What are the divine missions, or the works of God?

The entire work of God is common to all three Divine Persons of the Trinity. The work of creation is the work of the Trinity, though attributed to the Father. Likewise, the work of Salvation is attributed to the Son and the work of sanctification is attributed to the Holy Spirit.

DIVINE WORK OF CREATION

What is the divine work of creation?

Creation is the work of God bringing into existence everything and everyone, seen and unseen, out of love and without any help.

Who are angels?

Angels are spiritual creatures who do not have bodies as humans do. Angels give glory to God without ceasing and sometimes serve God by bringing his message to people.

Who is the human person?

The human person is uniquely created in the image and likeness of God. Human dignity is fulfilled in the vocation to a life of happiness with God.

What is the soul?

The soul is the spiritual part of a person. It is immortal; it never dies. The soul is the innermost being, that which bears the imprint of the image of God.

What is the intellect?

The intellect is an essential power of the soul. It is the power to know God, yourself, and others; it is the power to understand the order of things established by God.

What is free will?

Free will is an essential quality of the soul. It is the God-given ability and power to recognize him as part of our lives and to choose to center our lives around him as well as to choose between good and evil. By free will, the human person is capable of directing oneself toward the truth, beauty and good, namely, life in communion with God.

What is Original Sin?

Original Sin is the sin of Adam and Eve by which they choose evil over obedience to God. By doing so, they lost the state of original holiness for themselves and for all their descendants. As a result of Original Sin, death, sin, and suffering entered into the world.

JESUS CHRIST, THE INCARNATE SON OF GOD

What is the Annunciation?

The Annunciation is the announcement by the angel Gabriel to Mary that God chose her to be the mother of Jesus, the Son of God, by the power of the Holy Spirit.

What is the Incarnation?

The word *incarnation* comes from a Latin word meaning "take on flesh." The term *Incarnation* is the event in which the Son of God, the Second Person of the Holy Trinity, truly became human while remaining truly God. Jesus Christ is true God and true man.

What does it mean that Jesus is Lord?

The word *lord* means "master, ruler, a person of authority" and is used in the Old Testament to name God. The designation, or title, "Jesus, the Lord" expresses that Jesus is truly God.

What is the Paschal Mystery?

The Paschal Mystery is the saving events of the Passion, Death, Resurrection, and glorious Ascension of Jesus Christ; the passing over of Jesus from death into a new and glorious life; the name we give to God's plan of Salvation in Jesus Christ.

What is Salvation?

The word *salvation* comes from a Latin word meaning "to save." Salvation is the saving, or deliverance, of humanity from the power of sin and death through Jesus Christ. All Salvation comes from Christ through the Church.

What is the Resurrection?

The Resurrection is the historical event of Jesus being raised from the dead to a new glorified life after his Death on the Cross and burial in the tomb.

What is the Ascension?

The Ascension is the return of the Risen Christ in glory to his Father, to the world of the divine.

What is the Second Coming of Christ?

The Second Coming of Christ is the return of Christ in glory at the end of time to judge the living and the dead; the fulfillment of God's plan in Christ.

What does it mean that Jesus is the Messiah?

The word *messiah* is a Hebrew term meaning "anointed one." Jesus Christ is the Anointed One, the Messiah, who God promised to send to save people. Jesus is the Savior of the world.

MYSTERY OF THE CHURCH

What is the Church?

The word *church* means "convocation," those called together. The Church is the sacrament of Salvation—the sign and instrument of our reconciliation and communion with God the Holy Trinity and with one another. The Church is the Body of Christ, the people God the Father has called together in Jesus Christ through the power of the Holy Spirit.

What is the central work of the Church?

The central work of the Church is to proclaim the Gospel of Jesus Christ and to invite all people to come to know and believe in him and to live in communion with him. We call this work of the Church "evangelization," a word that comes from a Greek word that means "to tell good news."

What is the Body of Christ?

The Body of Christ is an image for the Church used by Saint Paul the Apostle that teaches that all the members of the Church are one in Christ, who is the Head of the Church, and that all members have a unique and vital work in the Church.

Who are the People of God?

The People of God are those the Father has chosen and gathered in Christ, the Incarnate Son of God, the Church. All people are invited to belong to the People of God and to live as one family of God.

What is the Temple of the Holy Spirit?

The Temple of the Holy Spirit is a New Testament image used to describe the indwelling of the Holy Spirit in the Church and within the hearts of the faithful.

What is the Communion of Saints?

The Communion of Saints is the communion of holy things and holy people that make up the Church. It is the communion, or unity, of all the faithful, those living on Earth, those being purified after death, and those enjoying life everlasting and eternal happiness with God, the angels, Mary and all the Saints.

What are the Marks of the Church?

The Marks of the Church are the four attributes and essential characteristics of the Church and her mission, namely, one, holy, catholic, and apostolic.

Who are the Apostles?

The word *apostle* comes from a Greek word meaning "to send away." The Apostles were those twelve men chosen and sent by Jesus to preach the Gospel and to make disciples of all people.

Who are the "Twelve"?

The "Twelve" is the term that identifies the Apostles chosen by Jesus before his Death and Resurrection. "The names of the twelve apostles are these: first, Simon called Peter, and his brother Andrew; James, the son of Zebedee, and his brother John; Philip and Bartholomew, Thomas and Matthew the tax collector; James the son of Alphaeus, and Thaddaeus; Simon the Cananean, and Judas Iscariot who betrayed him" (Matthew 10:2–4). The Apostle Matthias was chosen after Jesus' Ascension.

What Is Pentecost?

Pentecost is the coming of the Holy Spirit upon the Church as promised by Jesus; it marks the beginning of the work of the Church.

Who are the ordained ministers of the Church?

The ordained ministers of the Church are those baptized men who are consecrated in the Sacrament of Holy Orders to serve the whole Church. Bishops, priests, and deacons are the ordained ministers of the Church and make up the clergy.

How do the Pope and other bishops guide the Church in her work?

Christ, the Head of the Church, governs the Church through the Pope and the college of bishops in communion with him. The Pope is the bishop of Rome and the successor of Saint Peter the Apostle. The pope, the Vicar of Christ, is the visible foundation of the unity of the whole Church. The other bishops are the successors of the other Apostles and are the visible foundation of their own particular Churches. The Holy Spirit guides the Pope and the college of bishops working together with the Pope, to teach the faith and moral doctrine without error. This grace of the Holy Spirit is called *infallibility*.

What is the consecrated life?

The consecrated life is a state of life for those baptized who promise or vow to live the Gospel by means of professing the evangelical counsels of poverty, chastity, and obedience, in a way of life approved by the Church. The consecrated life is also known as the "religious life."

Who are the laity?

The laity (or laypeople) are all the baptized who have not received the Sacrament of Holy Orders nor have promised or vowed to live the consecrated life. They are called to be witnesses to Christ at the very heart of the human community.

THE BLESSED VIRGIN MARY

What is Mary's role in God's loving plan for humanity?

Mary has a unique role in God's plan of Salvation for humanity. For this reason she is full of grace from the first moment of her conception, or existence. God chose Mary to be the mother of the Incarnate Son of God, Jesus Christ, who is truly God and truly man. Mary is the Mother of God, the Mother of Christ, and the Mother of the Church. She is the greatest Saint of the Church.

What is the Immaculate Conception?

The Immaculate Conception is the unique grace given to Mary that totally preserved her from the stain of all sin from the very first moment of her existence, or conception, in her mother's womb and throughout her life.

What is the perpetual virginity of Mary?

The *perpetual virginity of Mary* is a term that describes the fact that Mary remained always a virgin. She was virgin before the conception of Jesus, during his birth, and remained a virgin after the birth of Jesus her whole life.

What is the Assumption of Mary?

At the end of her life on Earth, the Blessed Virgin Mary was taken body and soul into Heaven, where she shares in the glory of her Son's Resurrection. Mary, the Mother of the Church, hears our prayers and intercedes for us with her Son. She is an image of the heavenly glory in which we all hope to share when Christ, her Son, comes again in glory.

LIFE EVERLASTING

What is eternal life?

Eternal life is life after death. At death the soul is separated from the body. In the Apostles' Creed we profess faith in "the life everlasting." In the Nicene Creed we profess faith in "the life of the world to come."

What is the particular judgment?

The particular judgment is the assignment given to our souls at the moment of our death to our final destiny based on what we have done in our lives.

What is the Last Judgment?

The Last Judgment is the judgment at which every human being will appear in their own bodies and give an account of their deeds. At the Last Judgment, Christ will show his identity with the least of his brothers and sisters.

What is the beatific vision?

The beatific vision is seeing God "face-to-face" in heavenly glory.

What is Heaven?

Heaven is eternal life and communion with the Holy Trinity. It is the supreme state of happiness—living with God forever for which he created us.

What is the Kingdom of God?

The Kingdom of God, or Kingdom of Heaven, is the image used by Jesus to describe all people and creation living in communion with God. The Kingdom of God will be fully realized when Christ comes again in glory at the end of time.

What is Purgatory?

Purgatory is the opportunity after death to purify and strengthen our love for God before we enter Heaven.

What is hell?

Hell is the immediate and everlasting separation from God.

LITURGY AND WORSHIP

What is worship?

Worship is the adoration and honor given to God. The Church worships God publicly in the celebration of the liturgy. The liturgy is the Church's worship of God. It is the work of the whole Church. In the liturgy the mystery of Salvation in Christ is made present by the power of the Holy Spirit.

What is the liturgical year?

The liturgical year is the cycle of seasons and great feasts that make up the Church's year of worship. The main seasons and times of the Church year are Advent, Christmas, Lent, Easter Triduum, Easter, and Ordinary Time.

THE SACRAMENTS

What are the Sacraments?

The Sacraments are seven signs of God's love and the main liturgical actions of the Church through which the faithful are made sharers in the Paschal Mystery of Christ. They are effective signs of grace, instituted by Christ and entrusted to the Church, by which divine life is shared with us.

What are the Sacraments of Christian Initiation?

The Sacraments of Christian Initiation are Baptism, Confirmation, and the Eucharist. These three Sacraments are the foundation of every Christian life. "Baptism is the beginning of new life in Christ; Confirmation is its strengthening; the Eucharist nourishes the faithful for their transformation into Christ."

What is the Sacrament of Baptism?

Through Baptism we are reborn into new life in Christ. We are joined to Jesus Christ, become members of the Church, and are reborn as God's children. We receive the gift of the Holy Spirit; and Original Sin and our personal sins are forgiven. Baptism marks us indelibly and forever as belonging to Christ. Because of this, Baptism can be received only once.

What is the Sacrament of Confirmation?

Confirmation strengthens the graces of Baptism and celebrates the special gift of the Holy Spirit. Confirmation also imprints a spiritual or indelible character on the soul and can be received only once.

What is the Sacrament of the Eucharist?

The Eucharist is the source and summit of the Christian life. In the Eucharist the faithful join with Christ to give thanksgiving, honor, and glory to the Father through the power of the Holy Spirit. Through the power of the Holy Spirit and the words of the priest, the bread and wine become the Body and Blood of Christ.

What is the obligation of the faithful to participate in the Eucharist?

The faithful have the obligation to participate in the Eucharist on Sundays and holy days of obligation. Sunday is the Lord's Day. Sunday, the day of the Lord's Resurrection, is "the foundation and kernel of the whole liturgical year." Regular participation in the Eucharist and receiving Holy Communion is vital to the Christian life. In the Eucharist we receive the Body and Blood of Christ.

What is the Blessed Sacrament?

The Blessed Sacrament is another name for the Eucharist. The term is often used to identify the Eucharist reserved in the tabernacle.

What is the Mass?

The Mass is the main celebration of the Church at which we gather to listen to the Word of God (Liturgy of the Word) and through which we are made sharers in the saving Death and Resurrection of Christ and give praise and glory to the Father (Liturgy of the Eucharist).

What are the Sacraments of Healing?

Penance and the Anointing of the Sick are the two Sacraments of Healing. Through the power of the Holy Spirit, Christ's work of Salvation and healing of the members of the Church is continued.

What is the Sacrament of Penance and Reconciliation?

The Sacrament of Penance and Reconciliation is one of the two Sacraments of Healing through which we receive God's forgiveness for the sins we have committed after Baptism.

What is confession?

Confession is the telling of sins to a priest in the Sacrament of Penance and Reconciliation. This act of the penitent is an essential element of the Sacrament. Confession is also another name for the Sacrament of Penance and Reconciliation.

What is the seal of confession?

The seal of confession is the obligation of the priest to never reveal to anyone what a penitent has confessed to him.

What is contrition?

Contrition is sorrow for sins that includes the desire and commitment to make reparation for the harm caused by one's sin and the purpose of amendment not to sin again. Contrition is an essential element of the Sacrament of Penance and Reconciliation.

What is a penance?

A penance is a prayer or act of kindness that shows we are truly sorry for our sins and that helps us repair the damage caused by our sin. Accepting and doing our penance is an essential part of the Sacrament of Penance and Reconciliation.

What is absolution?

Absolution is the forgiveness of sins by God through the ministry of the priest.

What is the Sacrament of the Anointing of the Sick?

The Sacrament of the Anointing of the Sick is one of the two Sacraments of Healing. The grace of this Sacrament strengthens our faith and trust in God when we are seriously ill, weakened by old age, or dying. The faithful may receive this Sacrament each time they are seriously ill or when an illness gets worse.

What is Viaticum?

Viaticum is the Eucharist, or Holy Communion, received as food and strength for a dying person's journey from life on Earth through death to eternal life.

What are the Sacraments at the Service of Communion?

Holy Orders and Matrimony are the two Sacraments at the Service of Communion. These Sacraments bestow a particular work, or mission, on certain members of the Church to serve in building up the People of God.

What is the Sacrament of Holy Orders?

The Sacrament of Holy Orders is one of the two Sacraments at the Service of Communion. It is the Sacrament in which baptized men are consecrated as bishops, priests, or deacons to serve the whole Church in the name and person of Christ.

Who is a bishop?

A bishop is a priest who receives the fullness of the Sacrament of Holy Orders. He is a successor of the Apostles and shepherds a particular Church entrusted to him by means of teaching, leading divine worship, and governing the Church as Jesus did.

Who is a priest?

A priest is a baptized man who has received the Sacrament of Holy Orders. Priests are coworkers with their bishops, who have the ministry of authentically teaching the faith, celebrating divine worship, above all the Eucharist, and guiding their Churches as true pastors.

Who is a deacon?

A deacon is ordained to assist bishops and priests. He is not ordained to the priesthood but to a ministry of service to the Church.

What is the Sacrament of Matrimony?

The Sacrament of Matrimony is one of the two Sacraments at the Service of Communion. In the Sacrament of Matrimony a baptized man and a baptized woman dedicate their lives to the Church and to one another in a lifelong bond of faithful life-giving love. In this Sacrament they receive the grace to be a living sign of Christ's love for the Church.

What are the sacramentals of the Church?

Sacramentals are sacred signs instituted by the Church. They include blessings, prayers, and certain objects that prepare us to participate in the sacraments and make us aware of and help us respond to God's loving presence in our lives.

THE MORAL LIFE

Why was the human person created?
The human person was created to give honor and glory to God and to live a life of beatitude with God here on Earth and forever in Heaven.

What is the Christian moral life?
The baptized have new life in Christ in the Holy Spirit. They respond to the desire for happiness that God has placed in every human heart by cooperating with the grace of the Holy Spirit and living the Gospel. The moral life is a spiritual worship that finds its nourishment in the liturgy and celebration of the Sacraments.

What is the way to happiness revealed by Jesus Christ?
Jesus taught that the Great Commandment of loving God above all else and our neighbor as ourselves is the path to happiness. It is the summary and heart of the Commandments and all of God's Law.

What are the Ten Commandments?
The Ten Commandments are the Laws of the Covenant that God revealed to Moses and the Israelites on Mount Sinai. The Ten Commandments are also known as the Decalogue, or "Ten Words." They are the "privileged expression of the natural law," which is written on the hearts of all people.

What are the Beatitudes?
The Beatitudes are the teachings of Jesus that summarize the path to true happiness, the Kingdom of God, which is living in communion and friendship with God, and with Mary and all the Saints. The Beatitudes guide us in living as disciples of Christ by keeping our life focused and centered on God.

What is the New Commandment?
The New Commandment is the Commandment of love that Jesus gave his disciples. Jesus said, "I give you a new commandment: love one another. As I have loved you, so you should also love one another" (John 13:34).

What are the Works of Mercy?
The word *mercy* comes from a Hebrew word pointing to God's unconditional love and kindness at work in the world. Human works of mercy are acts of loving kindness by which we reach out to people in their corporal and spiritual needs.

What are the precepts of the Church?
Precepts of the Church are specific responsibilities that concern the moral Christian life united with the liturgy and nourished by it.

HOLINESS OF LIFE

What is holiness?
Holiness is the state of living in communion with God. It designates both the presence of God, the Holy One, with us and our faithfulness to him. It is the characteristic of a person who is in right relationship with God, with people, and with creation.

What is grace?
Grace is the gift of God sharing his life and love with us. Categories of grace are sanctifying grace, actual grace, charisms, and sacramental graces.

What is sanctifying grace?
The word *sanctifying* comes from a Latin word meaning "to make holy." Sanctifying grace is a gratuitous gift of God, given by the Holy Spirit, as a remedy for sin and the source of holiness.

What is actual grace?
Actual graces are the God-given divine helps empowering us to live as his adopted daughters and sons.

What are charisms?
Charisms are gifts or graces freely given to individual Christians by the Holy Spirit for the benefit of building up the Church.

What are sacramental graces?
Sacramental graces are the graces of each of the Sacraments that help us live out our Christian vocation.

What are the Gifts of the Holy Spirit?
The seven Gifts of the Holy Spirit are graces that strengthen us to live our Baptism, our new life in Christ. They are wisdom, understanding, right judgment (or counsel), courage (or fortitude), knowledge, reverence (or piety), wonder and awe (or fear of the Lord).

What are the Fruits of the Holy Spirit?
The twelve Fruits of the Holy Spirit are visible signs and effects of the Holy Spirit at work in our life. They are charity (love), joy, peace, patience, kindness, goodness, generosity, gentleness, faithfulness, modesty, self-control, and chastity.

THE VIRTUES

What are virtues?
The virtues are spiritual powers or habits or behaviors that help us do what is good. The Catholic Church speaks of Theological Virtues, Moral Virtues, and Cardinal Virtues.

What are the Theological Virtues?

The Theological Virtues are the three virtues of faith, hope, and charity (love). These virtues are "gifts from God infused into the souls of the faithful to make them capable of acting as his children and of attaining eternal life" (CCC 1813).

What are the Moral Virtues?

The Moral Virtues are "firm attitudes, stable dispositions, habitual perfections of intellect and will that govern our actions, order our passions, and guide our conduct according to reason and faith. They make possible ease, self-mastery, and joy in leading a morally good life" (CCC 1804).

What are the Cardinal Virtues?

The Cardinal Virtues are the four Moral Virtues of prudence, justice, fortitude, and temperance. They are called the Cardinal Virtues because all of the Moral Virtues are related to and grouped around them.

What is conscience?

The word *conscience* comes from a Latin word meaning "to be conscious of guilt." Conscience is that part of every human person that helps us judge whether a moral act is in accordance or not in accordance with God's Law; our conscience moves us to do good and avoid evil.

MORAL EVIL AND SIN

What is moral evil?

Moral evil is the harm we willingly inflict on one another and on God's good creation.

What is temptation?

Temptation is everything, either within us or outside us, that tries to move us from doing something good that we know we can and should do and to do or say something we know is contrary to the will of God. Temptation is whatever tries to move us away from living a holy life.

What is sin?

Sin is freely and knowingly doing or saying that which is against the will of God and the Law of God. Sin sets itself against God's love and turns our hearts away from his love. The Church speaks of mortal sin, venial sin, and Capital Sins.

What is mortal sin?

A mortal sin is a serious, deliberate failure in our love and respect for God, our neighbor, creation, and ourselves. It is knowingly and willingly choosing to do something that is gravely contrary to the Law of God. The effect of mortal sin is the loss of sanctifying grace and, if unrepented, mortal sin brings eternal death.

What are venial sins?

Venial sins are sins that are less serious than a mortal sin. They weaken our love for God and for one another and diminish our holiness.

What are Capital Sins?

Capital sins are sins that are at the root of other sins. The seven Capital Sins are false pride, avarice, envy, anger, gluttony, lust, and sloth.

CHRISTIAN PRAYER

What is prayer?

Prayer is conversation with God. It is talking and listening to him, raising our minds and hearts to God the Father, Son, and Holy Spirit.

What is the prayer of all Christians?

The Lord's Prayer, or Our Father, is the prayer of all Christians. It is the prayer Jesus taught his disciples and gave to the Church. The Lord's Prayer is "a summary of the whole Gospel." Praying the Lord's Prayer "brings us into communion with the Father and his Son, Jesus Christ" and develops "in us the will to become like [Jesus] and to place our trust in the Father as he did" (CCC 2763).

What are the traditional expressions of prayer?

The traditional expressions of prayer are vocal prayer, the prayer of meditation, and the prayer of contemplation.

What is vocal prayer?

Vocal prayer is spoken prayer; prayer using words said aloud.

What is the prayer of meditation?

Meditation is a form of prayer in which we use our minds, hearts, imaginations, emotions, and desires to understand and follow what the Lord is asking us to do.

What is the prayer of contemplation?

Contemplation is a form of prayer that is simply being with God.

What are the traditional forms of prayer?

The traditional forms of prayer are the prayers of adoration and blessing, the prayer of thanksgiving, the prayer of praise, the prayer of petition, and the prayer of intercession.

What are devotions?

Devotions are part of the prayer life of the Church and of the baptized. They are acts of communal or individual prayer that surround and arise out of the celebration of the liturgy.

BOOKS of the BIBLE

The Old Testament

Law (Torah) or Pentateuch

Genesis	(Gn)
Exodus	(Ex)
Leviticus	(Lv)
Numbers	(Nm)
Deuteronomy	(Dt)

Historical Books

Joshua	(Jos)
Judges	(Jgs)
Ruth	(Ru)
First Book of Samuel	(1 Sm)
Second Book of Samuel	(2 Sm)
First Book of Kings	(1 Kgs)
Second Book of Kings	(2 Kgs)
First Book of Chronicles	(1 Chr)
Second Book of Chronicles	(2 Chr)
Ezra	(Ezr)
Nehemiah	(Neh)
Tobit	(Tb)
Judith	(Jdt)
Esther	(Est)
First Book of Maccabees	(1 Mc)
Second Book of Maccabees	(2 Mc)

Poetry and Wisdom Books

Job	(Jb)
Psalms	(Ps)
Proverbs	(Prv)
Ecclesiastes	(Eccl)
Song of Songs	(Sg)
Wisdom	(Wis)
Sirach/Ecclesiasticus	(Sir)

Prophets

Isaiah	(Is)
Jeremiah	(Jer)
Lamentations	(Lam)
Baruch	(Bar)
Ezekiel	(Ez)
Daniel	(Dn)
Hosea	(Hos)
Joel	(Jl)
Amos	(Am)
Obadiah	(Ob)
Jonah	(Jon)
Micah	(Mi)
Nahum	(Na)
Habakkuk	(Hb)
Zephaniah	(Zep)
Haggai	(Hg)
Zechariah	(Zec)
Malachi	(Mal)

The New Testament

The Gospels

Matthew	(Mt)
Mark	(Mk)
Luke	(Lk)
John	(Jn)

Early Church

Acts of the Apostles	(Acts)

Letters of Paul and Other Letters

Romans	(Rom)
First Letter to the Corinthians	(1 Cor)
Second Letter to the Corinthians	(2 Cor)
Galatians	(Gal)
Ephesians	(Eph)
Philippians	(Phil)
Colossians	(Col)
First Letter to the Thessalonians	(1 Thes)
Second Letter to the Thessalonians	(2 Thes)
First Letter to Timothy	(1 Tm)
Second Letter to Timothy	(2 Tm)
Titus	(Ti)
Philemon	(Phlm)
Hebrews	(Heb)
James	(Jas)
First Letter of Peter	(1 Pt)
Second Letter of Peter	(2 Pt)
First Letter of John	(1 Jn)
Second Letter of John	(2 Jn)
Third Letter of John	(3 Jn)
Jude	(Jude)

Revelation

Revelation	(Rv)

GLOSSARY

A — B

aggiornamento *page 13*

This Italian word means "bring up to date" and was used by Pope John XXIII to describe the work of the Second Vatican Council.

apostate(s) *page 90*

A person who renounces a religious belief is referred to as an apostate. Throughout Church History, apostates have rejected various doctrines of the Catholic Church.

apostolic succession *page 50*

The unbroken connection between the Popes and bishops with the Apostles is called the apostolic succession; bishops are the successors of the Apostles.

Baptism *page 112*

This Sacrament of Christian Initiation celebrates a spiritual birth into new life in Christ. The baptized is joined to Jesus Christ, becomes a member of the Church, and is reborn as God's adoptive child. At Baptism, the gift of the Holy Spirit is received, and Original Sin and personal sins are forgiven.

C — D

celibacy *page 152*

The state of not being married is celibacy, which assumes chaste living.

charism(s) *page 12*

These graces or gifts are given by the Holy Spirit to build up the Church on Earth for the good of all people and the needs of the world.

Christendom *page 91*

During this period of Church History, the Church grew in territory and in both temporal and spiritual authority resulting in the Pope's authority exceeding that of the emperors and kings in Western Civilization.

Confirmation *page 112*

The Sacrament of Christian Initiation completes Baptism and celebrates the special gift of the Holy Spirit sealed upon one who is confirmed.

conjugal act *page 148*

According to God's plan for life and love, the unique expression of sexual love between a husband and a wife who freely give their whole selves to each other is the conjugal act.

consecrated life *page 27*

The life of the baptized who promise or vow to live the evangelical counsels of poverty, chastity, and obedience in a way of life approved by the Church is the consecrated life.

constitutions *page 15*

A constitution is a formal and official declaration of basic principles of a particular group. Church teaches from various teaching documents, one of them being constitutions.

contemplation *page 52*

This form of prayer is simply time spent focusing only being with God.

conversion *page 135*

Based on a word meaning "turning away," a conversion is the turning of one's heart back toward God and away from that which weakens our friendship with him.

E — F — G — H

ecumenism *page 48*

The dedicated search to draw all Christians together to manifest the unity that Christ wills for his Body, the Church, on Earth is called ecumenism.

Eucharist *page 124*

This Sacrament of Christian Initiation celebrates our sharing in the Paschal Mystery, in which we receive the Body and Blood of Christ. Based on the Greek word for "gratitude," this term emphasizes our giving thanks to God in the liturgy.

free will *page 138*

The ability and power given to us by God to choose between good and evil is free will. God created us to use our free will to recognize him as part of our lives and to choose to center our lives around him.

grace *page 102*

The gift of God sharing his life with us is called grace.

I — J — K — L

icon(s) *page 76*

An image or picture of Christ, Mary, a Saint, or an angel aiding in prayer is an icon.

infalliblity *page 51*

This charism of the Holy Spirit is given to the Church to guarantee that the official teaching of the Pope, or Pope and bishops, on matters of faith and morals is without error.

laity *page 26*

Those baptized members of the Church who have not received Ordination nor promised to live the consecrated life are part of the laity of the Church, or laypeople.

liturgical year *page 104*

This cycle of seasons, feasts and periods of sacred time make up the Church's year of worship.

liturgy *page 75*

The liturgy is the Church's worship of God using formal prayerful words and actions.

M — N — O — P

Magisterium *page 51*

The teaching authority and office of the Church, guided by the Holy Spirit, to authentically and accurately interpret the Word of God in Scripture and Tradition is the Magisterium.

meditation *page 52*

This form of prayer is using one's mind, heart, imagination, emotions, and desires to understand and follow the calling of the Lord.

memorial *page 124*

This term is used by the Church to signify that the Eucharist makes present and does not simply recall the past events of the Paschal Mystery.

mendicant *page 92*

Based on the Latin word for "to beg," this kind of person dedicates themselves to living the Gospel ideals of poverty. Mendicants rely on the generosity of others to support the work of evangelization.

mystery of faith *page 36*

This term describes the reality that we can never fully comprehend or fully grasp God or his loving plan for us.

ordained ministry *page 27*

These ministrial offices are related to the Sacrament of Holy Orders; the ministry of bishops, priests, and deacons.

Q — R — S

rite(s) *page 75*

The official words and formal actions used in the celebration of the liturgy are part of the rite; also refers to the entire liturgical celebration of a particular Sacrament.

sacrament *page 40*

An efficacious sign of grace, instituted by Christ and entrusted to the Church, by which divine life is shared with the faithful is a sacrament.

Sacraments of Christian Initiation *page 112*

These first three Sacraments of the Church are Baptism, Confirmation, and the Eucharist. One who receives all three Sacraments is fully initiated into the life of the Church.

sacrifice *page 125*

The free offering of oneself out of love for something of great value or for another is a sacrifice.

seal of confession *page 139*

Also known as the sacramental seal, this is the priest's obligation to keep absolutely secret what a penitent has told him in the Sacrament of Penance and Reconciliation.

T — U — V — W — X — Y — Z

vocal prayer *page 52*

This type of prayer uses spoken words, said aloud or in the quiet of one's heart.

INDEX

CREDITS